A HOME
in bloom

FOUR ENCHANTED
SEASONS WITH FLOWERS

CHRISTIE PURIFOY

HARVEST HOUSE PUBLISHERS
EUGENE, OREGON

For my mother,
Lexie Day

CONTENTS

What Makes a House a Home?

———————+———————

As a writer, I studiously avoid clichés, but phrases become overfamiliar and overused for a reason. If we ignore or discard them, we may lose something of great value. *What makes a house a home?* What brings the flat, material reality of a roof over our head and four walls around us to vivid life? The answers sometimes feel as trite as the question. You can find them splashed across a hundred items of home decor, from coffee mugs to art prints: *Live! Laugh! Love!* And yet these answers are anything but trivial. In fact, they are so meaningful they invite further questions: Can we really breathe life into the bricks and mortar of an ordinary house? Is there joy to be found in the sometimes tedious rhythms of our days? And how do we fill our shared spaces with love? Not just in theory but in practice? These are questions worth asking, and these are answers worth seeking, but they have led me, year after year, in season and out, to one surprising place—my garden.

For ten years, I have asked these questions and sought these answers on behalf of a red brick farmhouse that sits in the middle of a typical suburban neighborhood in the rolling, green countryside of Pennsylvania. But I asked the same questions when I lived in a tiny cookie-cutter apartment in small-town East Texas, and again in a high-rise apartment in the South Side of Chicago, and yet again in a seashell-stuccoed house in suburban North Florida. In each of these very different homes, I found that when I lived according to the seasonal rhythms of nature and when I worked to erase the dividing line between inside and outside, houses really did become homes and bricks and mortar bloomed as surely as the pink geraniums I once tended in a third-floor window box overlooking Forty-Eighth Street in Chicago.

The writer and Kentucky farmer Wendell Berry has famously insisted that there is no such thing as an "unsacred" place. He says there are only two categories of place: "sacred" places and "desecrated" places.[1] That word *desecrated* conjures bleak landscapes scarred by war or natural disaster, yet I think it also applies to the kinds of contemporary landscapes with which most of us are familiar: the asphalt sprawl of the suburbs, the chemical-dusted fields of modern agribusiness, the proliferation of chain stores that make it hard to tell the difference between one city and another. We are so accomplished at making functional places for waiting, for passing through, and for consuming, but how do we make places able to embrace the fullness of our human selves? We all know how dead we feel after too many minutes in a sun-deprived waiting room, or too many hours in stop-and-go traffic, or too many moments in the anonymous crowds of the food courts and shopping malls. What if our homes could be places that brought us back to life? For that is what sacred places do. They restore us and renew us and resurrect our spirits. They help us reconnect to our own souls, to other souls, and to the living ground beneath our feet. And they do this because, in some sense, they are themselves *alive*.

When I was a girl, I loved to read and reread The Chronicles of Narnia by C.S. Lewis. I wanted so much to believe that Narnia was a real place and that—maybe, just maybe—I might get there one day. I suppose my own kids might have felt that way about Hogwarts and nurtured secret hopes of an acceptance letter like Harry Potter's on their own eleventh birthday. And really, is that too much to want? Just an ordinary life with a bit more magic in it? When I longed for Narnia

to be real, it wasn't because I wanted to practice swordplay with a mouse or eat a sticky marmalade roll with a beaver. I understand now that what I wanted were forests where the trees are my friends. I wanted feasts where everyone I loved gathered around a table for good food and shared joy. I wanted a life that was also a quest, with shape and direction and meaning, like a voyage to the dawn.

I've recently been reading the Narnia stories to my youngest child, and it has only now occurred to me that the Narnia held frozen by the White Witch's spell is *not* an enchanted place. It is a nearly dead place, asleep under all that snow. It is beautiful at times, but it is the cold and terrible beauty of the witch herself. There is no birdsong, and there is no *life*. When Aslan returns, the spell breaks, and Narnia is re-enchanted. The whole country comes awake again, and the trees clap their hands for sheer happiness. It is a little like the words we read in an ancient song from *our* world: "Let the fields be jubilant, and everything in them; let all the trees of the forest sing for joy" (Psalm 96:12). That a place can be alive with spiritual presence is an old pagan concept, but it is also a Christian idea. The difference is that the Christians, like the true Narnians of Lewis's books, don't bow to the spirit in the tree; they join the praises of the trees and worship the Creator of all.

What makes a house a home? If the stories are to be believed, then a house becomes a home when it is brought to life like a velveteen rabbit, when it has a bit of extra magic like Hogwarts Castle, and when its purpose and aim is as clear as the dawn sought by Prince Caspian's voyaging ship. And it isn't only our children's stories that communicate this wisdom. The architect Christopher Alexander was well known for his insistence that good designs aren't those that merely look good on the pages of a magazine (or, I might add, in the little squares on Instagram or Pinterest) but are those that feel alive. *Aliveness* is his term for what he called "the quality that has no name," which he also described as a kind of "wholeness," "spirit," or "grace." [2]

I am not an architect, and I have little fluency in the languages of engineering and construction, but Alexander extended his own architectural mission to include each one of us when he described this earth as "the garden in which we live." For our own sake and for the sake of the place created to be our home, "we must choose to be gardeners. We must choose to make the garden beautiful." He said even actions as small as planting a flower can be a form of worship and insisted that the presence of God "comes to life and shines forth when we treat the garden properly."[3] I know he's right because I've seen it with my own eyes.

If the whole earth is a garden, then our homes are also gardens within a garden. Yet we are used to thinking of a garden as an accessory to a house. It is a bonus. An extra. It is "curb appeal." But gardens are much more than backdrops. They are much more than pretty pictures. Gardens are where our food comes from. Gardens are where beauty grows. Gardens are shelter. Gardens are also sacred spaces for private prayer and community celebration. Gardens are where we walk with God and work our muscles. They are living works of art. What if you could live in a painting? What if you could stroll through a song? What if you entered a chapel or even a cathedral every time you went out to fetch the mail? A home in bloom is not a static thing, and it is not a barren place. It is constant change as seasons shift and children grow, and it is continuous return as the peonies bloom every spring and likely will for a hundred years to come. A home in bloom is hard work at times, but it is the most satisfying, productive kind of work when anxieties slip from our shoulders with the rhythm of our rake or as each seed falls from our fingers.

If you long for beauty in a world that rarely has time for such nonsense, then consider this permission to pursue nonsense. Truthfully, it is the most important and most serious kind of nonsense—it is the nonsense of fairy tales and poetry and flower gardens. Brought together, house and garden tell a better story than either one alone. And they can even help us to live a better story. It is a story in

tune with the earth and with the music of the trees. It is a universal story yet highly personal and particular, never quite the same from one place to the next. I am tending an utterly unique story here at an old farmhouse in Pennsylvania, for these clods of clay soil, these red bricks, and these exact plants are found only here. And you, too, are invited to care for the particular ground beneath your feet in order to tell your own, entirely singular, home story.

If tending a garden is one way of re-enchanting our homes and bringing them to life, then we are like magicians. It is magic to plant an acorn and watch an oak tree grow. In fact, this is such an accessible form of magic that even the squirrels can do it. It is magic to grow flowers in a window box. It is magic to add a vase of daffodils to the breakfast table and completely alter the mood of the morning. It is magic to water the houseplants and feel our worries slip away. It is magic to order our daily lives with beautiful rhythms of work and rest, worship and play, cultivation and harvest. We aren't Aslan singing Narnian flora and fauna into being, but we too sing—and what happens when we do?

When we bring a branch of autumn leaves indoors in October or tend a bright pink geranium on the windowsill in January, we erase the dividing line between indoors and out, and in these small, ordinary ways we create a space for communion. Seen in this light, garden tasks can become some of the sustainable rhythms of a good life, rather than tedious chores or even entertaining hobbies. This book is your invitation to cultivate a way of life that is rooted in the vitality of a garden. There will be triumphs. There will be failures. There will be ordinary, daily miracles. But in all of it, and in every season, we will be growing a house into a home in bloom.

PART ONE

AUTUMN

BEGINNING
WITH THE END

———————————|———————————

Why begin a garden book in autumn? Why begin when evenings are drawing in and the trees are going bare? Spring is surely the more obvious choice: for instance, that moment in March or April in my own garden at Maplehurst when a green flush suddenly spreads across the landscape and dormant branches cry out almost overnight with blossom. Surely that is the true beginning of the garden year? It certainly feels that way when new life (and, yes, new weeds) are springing up all around. And yet the growth of a garden, like the progress of a year, is circular. We can touch it almost anywhere and find both beginning and end. Even a single seed tipped out from a paper packet is both a beginning and an end; it is the very first stage of a new plant and the final offering of a vanished fruit.

But enough poetry—let us talk of practicality. Autumn, it turns out, is the very best time of year for planting, despite the fact that garden centers seem to spend all their advertising power on bringing us through the doors in spring. This may be because plants are an easier sell in April. Who can turn away from a potted tulip in bloom or a crab apple tree in flower? Who among us isn't itching for a little time outdoors after a long winter spent inside? By the time autumn rolls around, I am sunburned and exhausted. I want only to turn the air-conditioning off and the woodstove on. I want a cup of tea and a good mystery novel by the fire, not a few more hours earning blisters at the end of a spade. The papery, onion-like exteriors of a tulip bulb are hardly beautiful enough to entice most of us outside for a spot of gardening on a blustery, mid-autumn day.

Which is a shame. Because the brilliant colors of the spring garden depend on a willingness to risk chapped hands and windburned cheeks in order to plant those bulbs six inches deep. April flowers rely on roots that go all the way back to October. And in fall, despite the weather fronts that begin to cool the air, the soil is still warm from the summer sun, and most plants will gladly sink their roots in deep with the help of more frequent autumn rains in order to burst out of the starting gate in spring. I have begun to shift more and more of my planting to fall. The weather for working outside is generally more reliable than the dizzying way spring careens between blizzards and heat waves. And by planting in fall, I have more time and energy for staying on top of the weeds in spring. After all, the pre-eminent garden task of spring is keeping up with the weeds until the perennials grow in enough to smother them out.

I might also have begun this book in January. That is the calendar new year after all, and it is always during that month after Christmas has been packed away that I really turn my attention to planning the next year's garden. But I have begun this book with autumn because it is all too easy to confine our gardening enthusiasm to spring. And a spring enthusiasm withers easily in the first heat wave of summer. When we plant in fall, we must wait quite a while to see the fruits of our efforts. The plants I buy from the clearance rack at the garden center this time of year do not look all that appealing. If the plant label has a photograph, then I study it, but usually I must ransack my memories for an image of this plant's spring flower and summer fullness and even its autumn color (for plants will not always color so well in a pot as in the ground). If we plant in autumn, then we spend winter nurturing the garden's greatest gift: hope. Our anticipation builds and builds until the day when we see the pink flowers on the 'Mohawk' viburnum

or the bracing lime green of the 'Ascot Rainbow' spurge, and the encounter means so much more than if we'd bought it ready-made in spring.

The pendulum swing between anticipation and fulfillment is the ticktock of my garden year. It is the heartbeat of my home. And it can become the particular rhythm of your own place. It is the movement between planting a container with strawberries and baking a pie. It is the dance of tipping bulbs into a trench and enjoying a child's teddy bear picnic among the daffodils. It is our comfort when the first flush of roses fades, because we know the scented lilies won't be far behind, and it is the reason we fill our windowsills with seedlings while the snow continues to fall outside. When we live according to the ebb and flow of a garden, we are gathering up our disparate days into something whole. No longer will winter cold feel meaningless (because we know peaches cannot grow on the tree we planted without a period of bracing cold—and besides, isn't the amaryllis flower by the window beautiful?). No longer will we resent the rain that interrupts our summer sun. ("Thank heavens!" we will say. "Now I have no need to water.") By embracing the rhythms of a garden year, we root ourselves more deeply in the present moment. It is a beautiful, life-giving paradox. And in this way, every ending will look to us like what it is: one more beginning and one more step toward new life.

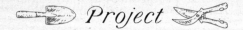

PLANT BULBS IN CONTAINERS

Spring-flowering bulbs planted in containers are easier to protect from squirrels and deer, and they are lovely to move around the house and garden for maximum enjoyment. I like to display potted bulbs on porch steps and gathered into groups on outdoor tables.

1. Gather your bulbs (anything from tulips and daffodils to crocus and Dutch iris), your containers (make sure they have good drainage—I like natural terra-cotta), and fresh potting soil (no need for fertilizers, but do make sure the soil mixture is very light, as bulbs can easily rot in heavy soil that stays wet).

2. Cover the drainage hole with mesh or a bit of broken clay so you don't lose too much soil when you water. Fill the pot with soil to within six inches or so of the top (leave more space for larger bulbs, less for smaller ones). Completely water the soil until saturated.

3. Fill your pot with bulbs very close together but not quite touching. Cover with additional soil, leaving an inch of space below the pot's rim.

4. Water thoroughly one more time. Label your bulbs!

5. Store your containers in a cold but not freezing place all winter. I use a garden shed, but an unheated garage also works well. You can leave them outdoors, perhaps sheltered against a warm wall and maybe covered with mulch.

6. In spring, check for signs of growth. As soon as growth begins, water well and place in a sunny spot.

THE CORNERS
OF A HOME

We cannot look at time. We cannot touch it or taste it or listen to it sing. Time has no scent, good or bad. And yet we do experience it. Mostly, we count it and track it and measure it. But what if, like mine, your brain is not hardwired for counting and tracking and measuring? What then? Though it is invisible and immaterial, I do visualize time through metaphor. It is a line spooling out like yarn in front of me. It is the firm, hard-packed road behind me. A day is a rhythm of three square meals, and the week is a series of seven blank boxes, like those "week at a glance" paper calendars I insist on using though I have a high-tech phone with a calendar app. A lifetime, I cannot really grasp. It is a mist. But a year within that life? Without question, a year is a perfect circle.

Until I look more closely. Then I see that it is a circle with corners. The year as I see it is an impossible shape. Circles do not have corners. Squares and rectangles and triangles do. Even a baby who lacks language but has dexterity with a shape-sorting toy knows that. Yet I am learning that impossible shapes become possible once we begin to see things that cannot be seen. Why shouldn't time made visible look like a circle with corners? The path that is summer is ending. The circle of the year has been feeling flat, but I can see a turn approaching. A bend in the road, a twist in the yarn, a shift in the light: here comes September.

Both of my daughters were born in September. In July of the year my firstborn daughter was eight, we packed up our Florida house for a move to Pennsylvania. Among our boxes was one filled with small wooden birdhouses I had purchased at a craft store. The birdhouses would be painted and decorated as fairy houses at a fairy-themed tea party birthday celebration for my girl's ninth birthday. I intended to set up those houses with paint and glue and dried flowers and Florida seashells on the front porch of our Pennsylvania farmhouse for third-grade classmates we didn't yet know. This was the most important box in our van. The second-most important box was labeled *baby girl clothes*. My fourth child, our second daughter, was due to be born two weeks after my oldest would turn nine. The year of the fairy house birthday was the last year I did not need to plan two birthday celebrations simultaneously. I went into labor three days after the party. Now I have two daughters with September birthdays only days apart.

September is the month of the year when the garden flatly refuses to stay outdoors. My daughters' birthday cakes are always decorated with garden flowers. Every countertop is spread with apples from our trees. I dry herbs, gathered from the raised bed just outside my kitchen door, by hanging bunches upside down in the pantry. The garden takes over the house because this is harvesttime. This is the fullness of summer. However, the corners of my rooms are filled with garden flowers at this time of year, more than any other, for one simple reason: I grow dahlias. Dahlias are late-summer bloomers, and I grow most of mine not as ornamental garden plants but as cut flowers. They are shrubby plants with hollow stems that cannot hold themselves up without the messy assistance of stakes and twine. There is no temptation to leave their blooms undisturbed to grow outdoors. In September, when they explode in flower, I cut them and bring them all inside where I fill myself up, up, up with their beauty as if filling a root cellar in my heart that I will pull from all winter long.

On roads and paths, corners are pass-through places. They are nothing more than the bend that carries us from what lies behind and on toward all that is yet

ahead. But if September is a corner of the year, as my mind insists on seeing it, then September is not an empty space to travel through. This corner catches me and holds me in a place of fullness. In September, I gather buckets of flowers. In September, we gorge ourselves on summer fruits even as the leaves of the crape myrtle trees outside the window begin turning to flame. In September, every corner of this house is filled to overflowing with earthly beauty.

There is beauty, but there is also this: in two different Septembers my daughters have been hospitalized. Late summer is a difficult time for those with allergies, with asthma, and with anxiety. Summer's abundance and its lack of school-day structure also has its shadow side. I can remember praying on two separate occasions for a daughter to be released from the hospital in time to celebrate her birthday at home. Two times that prayer has been answered with a yes. Illness, pain, suffering: these things catch us. They keep us from rushing ahead. But if September has a shadow side, illness has a silver lining: we are forced to pause and forced to be present. In a way, time stops—or at the very least, slows down. And without our stories of sickness, we would have no tales to tell of healing.

September is a corner I have never been able to take at full speed. It is simply too full. There has been too much sorrow and too much joy, and even during more straightforward Septembers I am slowed by the weight of memory. I am slowed by the heft of this bucket filled with water. The dahlias are coming on fast, and knowing that the first frost will finish them, I am stuck here in the garden, cutting stems as if the ephemeral lives of flowers were worth more than gold. A corner is the one place on the road where you are almost forced to look both ahead and behind. In fact, when the road bends there is less distance between ahead and behind, as if past and present draw nearer to one another in this strange turning point. When I imagine myself navigating the shift that is September, I am at the wheel of a car, turning right and seeing the road ahead and—just there at the edge of my shoulder—the road I have already traveled.

September is a hairpin turn, and everything, not just the road, seems doubled. It is summer fruit and autumn leaves. It is one daughter and then another. It is coming to this house nine years ago and celebrating a ninth birthday. It is now another ninth birthday coming round the bend.

I once took a birthday portrait of my youngest. She was seated in an armchair in our dining room, and she held one enormous stem from a 'Cafe au Lait' dahlia in her hand. In the photo, you cannot see her face. There is her hair and her sweet little-girl body, almost swallowed up by the chair, but instead of eyes, instead of nose, there is a swirl of rosy-beige petals. In the picture, she is four years old, she is just home from the hospital, and she is a dahlia child. In the Bible, we are reckoned to be like "flowers of the field." It is not exactly a compliment. On our own, our faithfulness to God is a fleeting thing. But I look at this photograph of my daughter and understand, just for a moment, something of the depth of God's love for us, his children.

Time is not itself a thing; it is a way of measuring and sifting. Like God in the beginning dividing heavens from earth and land from sea, we use our calendars and our ticking clocks to separate and categorize. With time as our tool, we bring order. We are better able to see and better able to understand because we have filtered the chaos. And year after year of Septembers have helped me see and understand. We separate and we gather in order to know what it is, exactly, that we have been given. What am I able to see and what am I able to understand through the lens of these days in particular? What do I see in these daughters, in these flowers, in these stories of hurt and hope and healing discovered in this corner of the year?

What I see most when I consider September is an invitation to reach out right now for all that is offered and for all that has returned. We pick no dahlias and decorate no birthday cakes in November or March. I can store up a harvest for winter, but I must gather it first. Apples left on the tree to rot will do me no good in January. And so in September I get up and I reach—for nourishment, for beauty, for love, and for every good gift that sits, perhaps unnoticed, in some corner of my home and of the year.

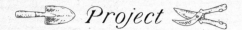

A CELEBRATION CAKE WITH FLOWERS

I love adding floral beauty to baked goods, especially celebratory cakes. A real flower is more beautiful than a buttercream flower *and* easier. While edible flowers are clearly a good idea, I also use nonedible flowers and simply cover the cake or wrap the stems, removing the flowers before slicing. For obvious reasons, I avoid using the flowers of poisonous plants. It's also best to use your own homegrown flowers so you know they haven't been sprayed with any chemicals. And finally, wash your flowers very well before using, otherwise you might find yourself singing about "itsy-bitsy spiders" instead of happy birthdays.

- *Edible flowers*: violets, violas (like Johnny-Jump-Up), pansies, nasturtium, flowering herbs (like chamomile, rosemary, and lavender), roses, lilac, hibiscus, mint leaves, blossoms from fruit trees, dandelion, honeysuckle, borage, elderberry flowers, squash blossoms, cornflowers, carnations, daylilies, scented geraniums, anise hyssop, sunflowers, dahlias, feverfew

- *Nonedible flowers to use with care*: tulips, peonies, calendula, cosmos, marigold

- *Flowers to avoid*: daffodil, lily of the valley, poisonous wild hemlock (which can look like Queen Anne's lace), poinsettia, azaleas, oleander, wisteria, sweet pea, mistletoe, holly, hydrangea, pokeweed, calla lily, iris, baby's breath, bleeding heart, foxglove, larkspur, morning glory

If in doubt? Don't use it or even touch it. Stick with varieties you know well and have grown yourself. Also keep in mind some flowers might be edible but not tasty. Do a bit more research to find the sweet petals that will taste good even if you don't remove them before eating.

More Tips

- Your cake will look beautiful for longer if your cut flowers are fully hydrated before using. Cut early in the morning and leave in cool water in a dark place for several hours before using. Do not add flower food to this water as you might for a bouquet.

- For larger flowers, leave a bit of stem in place. Push the stem into the cake for added stability.

- For nonedible or bitter-tasting flowers, cover the top of your cake with a circle of plastic wrap or parchment paper. Add flowers to fully cover the parchment paper, securing each bloom in place with a bit of frosting. Or wrap the stems with plastic wrap before pushing into the cake.

- For all flowers, cut away pollen-bearing stamens before using. A pollen-dusted cake might look pretty, but it's probably not a good idea for your guests with allergies.

FOUNDATIONS
TO GROW ON

———————+———————

A house without a foundation is like a tree without roots. That is to say, impossible. Foundations may be poured concrete or concrete block. They might be stone. There might be wood involved, but that wood is no longer alive, and so it must be protected from contact with the soil, or it will rot. Many of the very old houses in my part of Pennsylvania have stone foundations that are quite beautiful. It would be a shame to cover them up with traditional foundation plantings. My own old house has a few areas of visible stone holding up the brick and wood of the three-story structure, and I have tried to keep from covering those areas entirely with plants. But most houses do not have beautiful foundations, and all houses benefit from something that will visually settle the house into the land around it. This is why gardening—especially in my own country—consists primarily in the designing and the tending of that green mustache of plant life circling the base of the house.

When I moved to Maplehurst, the foundation borders around the front porch and the side walls were filled with variegated boxwood shrubs in pyramid shapes, lime-green hostas that sent out tall, heavily scented white flowers in late summer, and the rough and outstretched evergreen arms of horizontal juniper. I was still very new to gardening at that time, and I was surprised how much work—weeding, mulching, filling in of gaps—even small foundation beds required. I added quite a few herbaceous perennials like astilbe and Japanese anemone and shrubs like hydrangea, and I kept on filling as if I could pour in so many plants that the weeds would simply vanish. But the weeds only grew up within my new plants and my old plants, and the mess was both visual and practical and somehow even emotional. I despaired every time I stepped outside the door. However, the scent of those white hosta flowers in late summer was astonishing, and we would scoot our front porch rocking chairs nearer to the edge just to breathe it in more deeply.

Meanwhile, my gardening time was needed in the vegetable garden and in the flower garden, and though I wished the garden around the house would always look neat and presentable, in truth, it rarely did. The whole experience was so frustrating that when we rerouted the driveway that had formerly circled the house, we tore out the old foundation beds, and I seeded ordinary lawn grass right up to the front porch and the stone foundations. It was like a fresh green palate cleanser for an overtired gardener, and I loved it for a single summer season. But in winter, mud around the house was a sucking, squelching problem, and we needed paths to carry our feet from car to front door, from driveway to patio, and so we brought in a landscape designer to help us with that work. His name was Pete, and in his design he planned foundation beds and told me I could fill them with shrubs and ornamental grasses and they would be both beautiful and easy to maintain. I was skeptical. I worried that even these not-too-enormous foundation beds would eat up plants (and thus eat up money) and also eat up time (spent weeding and mulching), and I hesitated. Eventually, I agreed to the plan, and Pete's team removed the grass, outlined beds and paths with rusty steel edging, and filled the paths with gravel (we could not afford stone but wanted something more suited to an old house than concrete pavers). Still, for one whole year I hesitated to plant anything in those beds. Instead, we covered them with pine straw mulch. It wasn't beautiful, but it was at least weed-free.

A house without a foundation is like a tree without roots. And a house without a garden, with only green mowed grass or mulch-blanketed beds, is an unenchanted house, and while I feared the messy abundance of a foundation garden, I knew my house was asking for it. I knew as well it would cost money. It would take time. There would be periods of heavy weeding. But maybe I could still do it differently? Not "tear it all out and plant lawn grass" differently, but maybe I could make a green garden that was more beautiful than lawn and more unique than a typical green mustache of shrubs, and maybe it could—in time—take care of itself. *Maybe?*

I am in the middle of that experiment. It is too early to declare victory. Of course, it is almost always too early to declare victory in a garden. I have at least (mostly) tamed the visual chaos by planting more of less. Instead of astilbe and hostas and anemones, variegated boxwood and juniper and hydrangea, annuals in summer and chrysanthemums in fall—and on and on in bits and bobs of everything—I have planted only boxwood and prairie dropseed grasses in the front border. There are taller pyramids of green boxwood in the back, and there are balls of green boxwood in the middle, and there is a double row of grasses in front. When the grasses bloom in late summer, the whole picture becomes quite beautiful and exciting, with the rising sun illuminating the tall prairie dropseed flowers like gold and the wind tossing them against the solid forms of the evergreen shrubs. So far, I have only pine straw mulch around the shrubs, but I have begun adding a groundcover layer of our native carex, the Pennsylvania carex that likes to grow in neat green clumps beneath oak trees in Pennsylvania forests. I have also dug in a few experimental plants of *Epimedium* 'Rubrum', which is a much nicer name for this creeping, red-tinged native than barrenwort. This fall, I have even attempted to add one more simple layer with the addition of some 'White Triumphator' tulip bulbs that I hope in spring will pull the white of the porch posts down to ground level.

This front foundation bed is, essentially, a green mustache like every other green mustache that ever was, though I believe the grasses do give it a bit more life and liveliness. Around the front steps, I have tried to draw attention to the entrance by adding in some purple-leaved ninebark shrubs. When you step back, it looks a bit like wine spilled on a dark green tablecloth. At least it does in my own poetic imagination. I also added some vertical accents in the form of Japanese hollies, and I let purple-flowering *Verbena bonariensis* seed itself around for excitement. I like to think that area around the steps shouts a bit louder now so that guests know here—right here by the spilled-wine shrubs and the purple flowers waving for attention like excited young children—is a threshold, a place that says "welcome."

Garden design is a language, and I am slowly learning to speak this unfamiliar tongue. The irony is that we can all hear this language intuitively even if we cannot always explain what we have heard. I have no doubt that visitors now hear something good when they stand on my front steps that they never could hear when all I had was a chaos of flowers and scent and weeds. We feel things with our bodies in different spaces even if we are only aware of it like an itch in a hard-to-reach place. The story of this new foundation garden is still being written, but I can see now that it is a story about simplicity, contrast, and layers. It is a green story that speaks in purple exclamation points. In spring, the white porch posts and white vase-shaped tulips will link the house with the ground around it. Next fall, the grasses will dance again, and I will weed again, but this simple story will by then, I pray, have grown into a song.

PANICLE HYDRANGEAS

Most of us know hydrangeas as the shrubs with blue or pink mophead flowers: blue flowers grow on acidic soil while alkaline soil produces pink flowerheads. But there are so many other hydrangea varieties to try, many of which are more likely to thrive in our gardens. Mophead hydrangeas (*Hydrangea macrophylla*) are very thirsty plants, and by July I often find them wilting in my own garden. Mopheads also bloom on old wood (branch growth from the previous year), which means that winter cold can kill the developing flower buds so that summer brings only green growth with few flowers.

Panicle hydrangeas (Hydrangea paniculata) handle sunshine and drought better than mopheads, and they bloom on new wood. This means you can cut them right down to the ground in late winter or early spring and still have abundant flowers in July. I like a large, statuesque hydrangea, so I prefer to cut mine back, not all the way to the ground but down to a sturdy framework of branches about two to three feet high. Read the descriptions carefully, and you'll find some panicle types that grow very tall and some delicate little shrubs just perfect for a tight space or container. Because panicle hydrangeas also appreciate more sunlight than other kinds, you can plant them amongst other sun-loving shrubs in your foundation beds.

SCIENTIFIC NAME:
Hydrangea paniculata

COMMON NAME:
Panicle hydrangea

FAVORITE VARIETIES:
'Limelight', 'Little Lime',
'Fire Light', 'Bobo', 'Vanilla Strawberry'

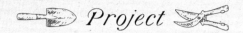 *Project*

DRYING HYDRANGEAS

Every September, I dry bunches of hydrangea flowers to keep me company in vases from autumn through spring.

1. Choose flowers that have already begun to dry a bit. Usually this means waiting until late summer or early fall.

2. Remove all green leaves.

3. Place your cut hydrangea flower stems in a vase with about an inch of water.

4. Do not add more water. The flowers will take up the water and then gently begin to dry as the vase goes dry. Once dry, remove them to a clean vase where they can stay all winter long.

5. Enjoy your dried hydrangeas on a mantelpiece or side table, or add dried flowers to an evergreen wreath.

BLUE ROSES

My father was a gardener, but I was not (I tried it one time after reading *The Secret Garden*, but the mosquitos were biting, so I went back inside). My father grew roses, and I sometimes cut them for the dinner table when asked by my mother, but I always cut them quickly because mosquitos feed in the dusky light before dinner. When I try to remember my father's roses, I see only daubs of color—as if my youngest daughter had reached into my mind with her paintbrush and *here!* a dash of coral and *there!* a splash of lemon yellow. I can't really see the flowers themselves. I can't tell you their shapes or recall the lines of their petals. They are a colorful blur in my mind, more like the memory of a feeling than the recollection of an actual thing.

The roses I remember best and see with utter clarity are the full, romantic, peach-colored roses on the wallpaper I chose for my bedroom the year I turned thirteen. I loved that wallpaper. I adored those roses. Cabbage roses, they're called. That isn't any kind of proper rose name, but it's a good word for roses that are fat and full and bursting as any garden-grown cabbages are bursting with rainwater in late summer. Cabbage roses are the opposite of florist roses. That, too, isn't a proper rose name, but it properly recalls the high and tight buds that never open and are mixed with a froth of baby's breath to be sold in plastic sleeves from supermarket shelves.

My first garden appeared as wallpaper in my bedroom with shades of warm peach and a contrasting border of dusty country blue. I have never seen a country-blue rose in real life, but I can say with certainty such roses once grew on my very own wall. I chose that wallpaper from a big book of wallpaper samples in a shop with my mother and sisters, but it is risky to redecorate one's bedroom at the transitional age of thirteen. By all rights, I should have hated that wallpaper by age sixteen. In three years, I leaped from polka dots and headbands to Doc Martens boots and flannel shirts. I traveled from top-forty countdowns on the radio to a stack of CDs from the Seattle alternative music scene. I should have despised those cabbage roses. I should have covered them with concert posters and photos of my swim team friends, but I did no such thing. I still loved those roses when, at eighteen, I traded that room for a bland cinderblock dormitory on a college campus. A few years later, when my former bedroom was given to my younger brother and the wallpaper removed, I knew two things absolutely: (1) the cabbage roses were no longer stylish and were certainly unsuitable for a high school boy, and (2) the room had been much more beautiful with that rose garden growing on the wall.

When I was a young girl, a few years before I chose that wallpaper, Laura Ashley floral-patterned dresses were all the rage, if one can use a word like *rage* to describe romance and nostalgia. Did Laura Ashley forever mold my aesthetic sensibilities? Or did I gravitate to Laura Ashley as strongly as I did because I thought flowers beautiful, and who wouldn't want to adorn themselves with beauty? It's a chicken-or-the-egg question. I don't know how to answer it except to say that Laura Ashley may have faded from style long before I reached adulthood, but I still seek out nostalgic floral patterns wherever I can find them. The year the British brand Liberty of London, famous for its crisp cotton fabrics with small-scale floral prints, launched a collection at Target, I set my alarm in order to shop when the sale first went live. I still have the sleeveless faux-silk shirt I bought that day. I've never really liked its ruffled collar, but I keep it and I wear it because the bright flower-meadow pattern makes me happy. I like nostalgic, romantic botanical prints. Always have. Always will.

Styles come and styles go, but those of us who love flowers are drawn to them whether they grow in gardens or spread across table linens or splash their happy pattern around our favorite rain boots. I have, since childhood, especially loved drawings and paintings of roses. I may have forgotten the visual details of my father's real garden roses, but I can still see my wall calendar from 1989; it had a different botanical print for every month, each in the style of Redouté, who is famously remembered for his portraits of Empress Josephine's roses. For months, I obsessively copied those botanical drawings with my colored pencils, and my mother even framed one of my imitations for her wall. At twelve years old, I wasted no time in my father's rose garden but gave everything to my attempts to capture the precise shadow of a curling rose petal like the one featured for the month of July.

Sometimes we cannot love a thing until art teaches us its value. A love for real roses is complicated by thorns and by the mosquitos so prevalent at dusk in central Texas in late spring. Even now, in Pennsylvania, my love of roses is complicated by the invasive Japanese beetles that devour the buds for nearly two months in midsummer. I don't think I could maintain my love for the real garden roses I tend today in my Pennsylvania garden if that love weren't continually fed by Dutch still-life paintings and William Morris wallpaper patterns and the scent of the perfume I most love to wear.

My own rational Western culture has a propensity to view the world only through the lens of a flat, material reality. We tend to categorize and sort everything with dualistic labels like *real* or *not real*, *fiction* or *nonfiction*, *true* or *false*. Real things are material things. Horses are real, but unicorns, so our thinking goes, are not. Garden roses in coral and lemon are real, but blue roses on wallpaper are not. Real things, we tell ourselves, have real value, and the rest is merely something "extra." An entertaining diversion, perhaps, though not necessary. But where does art fall in these dualistic categories? If unicorns are not real, what do we make of the medieval unicorn tapestry at the Cloisters in New York City? Why does its antique beauty make me want to cry? Of what significance are the unicorns rendered in crayon and marker that paper my young daughter's bedroom walls? In my own home, unicorns are arguably more real than horses.

Those categories of real and not real are valuable, but they are also limiting. They can make it more difficult for us to appreciate the necessity of art and symbol. They can make it harder for us to see the spiritual dimension of material reality. Because I have cultivated a love of roses over a lifetime, I know that a rose is so much more than the bug-eaten specimen I might pick from my garden on any given day. Roses are real in more ways than one. The Romantic poets famously emphasized a vision of the more that lay beyond our visible reality through symbolism, and one of their most beloved symbols was that of the blue flower. For writers like Novalis, the blue flower symbolized the creative pursuit of the infinite and unreachable. With solid words they expressed a longing for intangible beauties. We experience such things in the natural world, but they are also somehow beyond the natural world. They are not finite, like the rose I hold in my hand.

Tending a garden is the single most important way I participate in the material reality of the natural world. Because I garden, I am not only an observer—I am an actor in this play. I am a singer in this choir. I have picked up my paintbrush and *here!* a dash of red rose and *there!* a line of purple catmint. But I also participate in the natural world by cultivating unreal flowers: in the wallpaper I chose for the kitchen here at Maplehurst, in the photographs I take in my garden, in the clothes I wear and the books I read. In all these ways, my love for plants and trees and their flowers grows, and because this love is so well-fed—with stories and art and objects of usefulness and objects of prettiness—it is stronger than heat waves, and stronger than mosquito bites, and stronger than even the longest, coldest winter. The more I feed my love of gardens (with potted plants on the

kitchen counter and the gravy boat on my Thanksgiving table and the painting that hangs over our bed), the more it seems as if the real flower—the one growing in my garden right now—is only one part of something bigger and real-er called *rose*. I can admire a perfect garden rose, and yet it will not perfectly fulfill my longing for the beauty that goes by the name of *rose*.

Am I longing for the flowers that might grow in heaven? I don't think that's quite the explanation. I think I am longing for the truest and most vividly real flowers of all: the flowers that grow in the garden where heaven meets earth. C.S. Lewis called himself "a votary of the Blue Flower" when he described the feeling of longing that beauty stirred up in him even as a child of six.[4] This seems the right description for my own child self who drew roses, and admired Laura Ashley dresses, and chose rose-patterned wallpaper not because she loved gardens but because she ached for beauty. I sometimes think all that admiration and all that creative longing was a prayer, and that prayer is answered every summer when my garden blooms and every winter when I sit by the fire beneath my green garden wallpaper. My longing for beauty has never been completely and fully met, yet I am filled with gratitude for the beauty that does regularly fill my life. My art making, my homemaking, and my garden making are my attempt to open up—always wider and wider—a doorway to that place where blue flowers grow. Not heaven. Not earth. But the place where the two meet as one.

Plant This

SELF-SOWING FLOWERS

Most of us will be familiar with the difference between annuals and perennials. Annuals like sunflowers will live their entire life cycle in one season: plant a sunflower seed in late spring, and you will have a dried-out flower full of new seeds by the end of summer. Perennials like peonies come back year after year with no need for replanting. But there is another type that bridges these two categories and brings a wonderful serendipity to our gardens: these are self-sowing or self-seeding plants. They may be annuals, they may be tender perennials (meaning they do not survive very cold winters), or they may simply be short-lived perennials, but no matter their botanical type, these are the flowers that cast their seeds around them in order to return in new places and in more abundant numbers next year. Once self-sowers are established in your soil, every year you will find yourself surprised by your own garden, as if—who knew!—our gardens were really alive.

Some of my favorites reseed themselves vigorously (like verbena, daucus, orlaya, and feverfew) while others (like verbascum and poppy) might need a little coaxing to establish themselves. Either way, the spontaneity of self-sowing flowers creates a garden that is harder to control but a lot more fun.

Feverfew

FAVORITE SELF-SOWING FLOWERS
Tall verbena (*Verbena bonariensis*)
Chocolate lace flower 'Dara' (*Daucus carota*)
'Lauren's Grape' poppy (*Papaver somniferum*)
Orlaya
Feverfew
Verbascum 'Southern Charm'
Viola 'Johnny-Jump-Up'
Anise hyssop

PART TWO

WINTER

A MANIFESTO
AGAINST SHORTCUTS

I n our modern hurry-scurry, hustle-bustle culture, the road not taken is likely to be the long way round. We love to take shortcuts. We seek out the undemanding and the quick. We value efficiency. I am no different. How many of my internet searches begin with *easy this* or *simple that*? But there is a difference between simple and simplified. Simple living is a beautiful thing, as we learn how to do more and buy less, as we weed out options and distractions in order to focus on the things that matter most to us. But simplified is more like the Bolognese sauce that comes together in thirty minutes rather than the one on the card handwritten by our neighbor's Italian grandmother that asks for six hours of our day and three different kinds of meat. The simplified sauce might be the right one to choose on a particular day, but we kid ourselves if we say they are the same.

Like many people my age, I never have enough hours in the twenty-four to cross every item off my list. If I were to answer every email, I would have no time for prayer. If I were to cook every single meal from scratch, I would have no time to read the bedtime story. If I grew every vegetable from seed, I would have no time to write books. In order to do some of what I want to do, I must multitask, I must look for shortcuts, I must find an easier way. But just as a shortcut through the grass becomes, over time, a habitual path of dirt, my tendency to choose easy has become a reflex I no longer think about and almost never deny. If I invite friends to dinner, of course I will choose the menu I've made a hundred times in under an hour. If I pick a bunch of flowers, of course I will pop them in a mason jar with little thought. If my daughter asks for a layer cake when I intended to pull ice cream from the freezer, I laugh and ask, "What if we added a cherry on top? Would that be good enough?"

Again and again I pursue the good enough, and these choices help keep my head above water—except it has been such a long time since I dove down deep. What beauty might lie in the depths like a pearl? What peace could I find in the underwater quiet? What mysteries have I forgotten after all these years of treading water? These questions feel more pressing as Advent carries us toward Christmas. The weeks of Advent are the traditional season of preparation for the Christmas feast. We prepare our hearts, we prepare our homes, we even prepare our freezers, slowly filling them with cookies and candies and other Christmas treats. If I am honest with myself, I know deep within that the feast I desire can't be achieved only through shortcuts. I want the special gingerbread cake I only make this time of year. I want to taste the real butter cookies, though I know the slice-and-bake supermarket version would take little time. I want to see the staircase twinkling with lights, though I can't forget it will require time in January to untangle them and return them to their basement boxes.

When our marriage was young and we had no children, Jonathan and I were invited to dinner by a couple who lived down the hall from us in our Chicago apartment building. These were the days when I was learning to cook recipes with five ingredients and little fat, so I was unprepared for the meal these neighbors set before us. Imagine immaculate white plates. Imagine swirls of sauce and scattered herbs. Hear the tapping of our spoons against the sugar crust of a crème brûlée before the plunge into custard cool as silk.

Now imagine the view I had in my chair at that table: just behind my host's head, I could see teetering piles of dishes and wobbly towers of dirty pots and

pans. I could see an overfull sink and counters spread with opened jars and half-chopped vegetables. I remember feeling shocked—shocked that the food was so delicious, shocked that the menu was so complex, and shocked that I was permitted to see the swath of destruction this feast had wrought in that tiny apartment kitchen.

After that dinner, I began to understand that I knew how to overindulge but I didn't know how to feast. I knew how to keep a tidy home, but I'd never really felt free to make a mess. I knew how to take shortcuts in the kitchen, but I had no idea it was possible to create edible art and serve it on a porcelain plate with a sprinkling of finely chopped, flat-leaf Italian parsley. In the decade that followed, I pursued real food. I surprised my friends with fresh profiteroles when most of us had only ever had the frozen version from Costco. I whipped up a batch of mayonnaise in the food processor my mother-in-law gave me and promptly decided that the jarred stuff I disliked should never be sold under the same name. I could hardly stand to spread store-bought mayo on my sandwich, but I dipped fresh snap peas in the homemade version and couldn't stop. I had beginner's luck with sourdough bread (a luck that has evaded me in recent years) and realized I'd never really tasted bread before. But so many of those experiences now sit far back in my past. When did I last lose myself in the process? When did I stop looking for the long, winding roads?

I suppose the answer is that I had more children, I took on more paid work, I moved into an old house where even the simple upkeep is never simple. I began growing dahlias and stopped growing carrots. We brought home a dog. We brought home a kitten. I didn't do anything wrong; I did a lot of things right. Yet I feel undernourished. I'm looking at the road less traveled—by me, by so many—and I can't be sure I won't regret that path. I can't even tell where it ends, but this winter, while the garden sleeps, I want to choose, at least occasionally, the longer and more uncertain way.

When shortcut paths become visible through erosion, they are called desire lines. Grass that has been packed down to dirt by many footsteps will often follow the shortest or easiest route between an origin and a destination. They can even be made by animals such as cattle as they move regularly toward their water source. Desire lines show where we *want* to go and *how* we want to go there, but as they become visible in the landscape, they also become self-perpetuating. Unless the area is fenced off, the grass will never grow back because when we see a path, we are inclined to take it. Maybe the true desire line is the one that remains invisible. Shortcuts are habitual for me, but I want the things that shortcuts aren't equipped to give. I want to move slowly. I want to enjoy the process. I want to give anticipation time to grow. I want complexity—of flavor, of appearance, of experience. I want the richness of a long simmer and the glory of a tall tree. I want the kind of roots that need long years to grow. Is it an oak tree you desire? Plant the acorn. Is it a beautiful, sugar-crusted gingerbread house? Make it without a kit. Is it a cut flower garden you want? Start your seeds while the snow still flies. Do less and live more.

WITCH HAZEL

With patience, even cold-climate gardeners can have flowering color outdoors in winter. Grown as large shrubs or small trees, witch hazels are spectacular on sunny winter days when nothing else seems alive. In shades of tawny orange and lemon yellow, the starlike flowers can even carry a gorgeous perfume. Plant your witch hazel against an evergreen backdrop or wherever the low winter sun will set its flowers blazing. I have the beloved hybrid *Hamamelis* x *intermedia* 'Jelena' planted at the front northeast corner of my house. That way I am sure to notice it with astonishment when it finally unfolds its flowers.

Witch hazels might not look like much the first few years after planting. I have a yellow-flowering variety that I almost dug out. For five years, it seemed like a failure, but this year it is a blaze of starry yellow against the dark night sky of the cypress behind it. Some garden beauties are expected. Of course the peonies will bloom! But others feel more precarious, more impossible, and more surprising with every return.

SCIENTIFIC NAME:
Hamamelis

COMMON NAME:
witch hazel

FAVORITE VARIETIES:
Hamamelis virginiana (the North American native), hybrid varieties of *Hamamelis* x *intermedia*, such as 'Jelena' and 'Diane'

BRINGING
IN THE GREENS

———————— + ————————

When I was a child, Christmas arrived in a box we brought down from the attic on the day after Thanksgiving. My sisters and I would unpack the box with our mother, and within an hour our house was transformed from ordinary to special, from pleasant to beautiful. And beauty—even then—was the song of my heart. Like my mother before me, I still keep a beautiful Christmas stored in cardboard boxes and plastic bins. Reaching into the depths of these familiar old containers, I find the nativity figures we'll place in a stable made by my husband from old wood he found in our barn. I retrieve the tiny wooden ornaments with intricate figures of people and animals that I bought for each child at Chicago's German-style Christkindlmarket. I am especially happy to greet once again the delicate brass angels who spin and ring their bells powered by the heat of four white candles. Beautiful things can be purchased from shops and from artisans and kept, year after year, in boxes with fading labels.

But what if I'm sick of shopping? What if I've run out of room for more boxes? Perhaps the answer is to unwrap an old holiday tradition called *bringing in the greens*. This Christmas tradition is rooted in ancient observances that embraced a sacred sense of the seasons. Branches, vines, and sprigs of evergreen plants— pine and cedar, holly and ivy, and even (perhaps in warmer climates) magnolia leaves and palm fronds—are used as Christmas decor. When we bring in the greens, we go outside and do quite literally that: we gather branches and swags of fresh, resinous, scented evergreen, and we bring the outside in. We bring Christmas in, because of course some deep part of Christmas must be too wild and mysterious to contain in boxes. It makes sense that we would need to go out in search of it.

Evergreens of all sorts are special this time of year because they remind us of the persistence of life even during dark winter seasons. They symbolize eternal life, and they are a traditional part of many Advent and Christmas celebrations, from wreaths to garlands to trees in homes and churches. Sadly, *symbol* has become a flat, paper-thin word for most of us. To say that evergreen boughs symbolize eternal life is to invoke dusty chalkboards, language exams, and graded essays. What do symbols have to do with our actual lives? After all, we are not like the Victorians sending coded messages in bouquets according to the symbolic language of flowers. We are not ancient pagans trying to manipulate our gods with mysterious woodland rites and holly wreaths. We are modern people who know there is nothing spiritually sacred about an ordinary leaf, and so we power our celebrations with batteries, electric power strips, and LED bulbs. Symbols are found in books and brains, not our homes. *Or are they?*

Are symbols merely the paper-thin mental processes I learned about in English class? Certainly to say that matter does not matter, that a leaf is no different from a battery, seems especially ironic at Christmastime. The mystery and wonder of the Christmas story—a story of incarnation, a story of God made flesh—belongs to the natural world as much as we ourselves belong to the natural world. We are makers, made in the image of a great Maker, but have we cluttered up our world so thoroughly with our mass-produced efforts that we have forgotten the significance of real, living things? I offer no diatribe against batteries and bulbs. I feel a certain nostalgic fondness for metallic tinsel. But symbols are signposts toward the most real things in our real world. To ignore them is to ignore that

which is most essential in life. For faith is not only a thought in our heads, but a way of faithfulness in the world, and it involves real bread and real wine, real wounds and real life. Such things are symbolic, which is to say they are more real than is at first apparent. They are real in visible *and* invisible ways.

On the surface, real evergreens don't seem as "everlasting" as faux, and their realness isn't always comfortable or convenient. Yes, they smell like heaven, but they sometimes make us sneeze. They can prick us with their spines or thorns. They dry out quickly and must be misted with water or kept in a vase. They force us to pay careful attention to the days. Bring in the greens too soon, and they will not last till Twelfth Night. But real greens are never packed up into boxes. They are never stored away in dusty attics or basements. Real Christmas greens are laid back outside, where they are transformed into soil that will one day feed spring flowers. What could be more everlasting than that?

Since moving to Maplehurst, I have made bringing in the greens a regular part of my family's preparation for Christmas. I love the walk outside in frosty air, sometimes with a willing child in tow, as I hunt for anything still green enough to bring inside. If it has red berries, all the better. I have even brought home fresh holly from the local winter farm market in order to drop sprigs in small bud vases I can tuck into all corners of the house. Bringing in the greens is one way I prepare for Christmas with my body. I have the pink in my cheeks and the scratches on my hands to prove it. Bringing in the greens is also one way I connect the celebrations happening inside my home with the created world outside. For Jesus came to save not just his people but this whole created world. Symbols, I am discovering, are not ideas to decode but invitations to experience. Can an ivy leaf or pine needle be a sacred thing? For those with eyes to see, they've never been anything else.

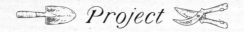 *Project*

A SIMPLE, NATURAL WREATH

Wreath making is an art, and an elaborate evergreen wreath with fresh and dried materials gathered from your own garden might be your "take the long road" winter project. For those of us who want to gather greens for wreaths but prefer to save time for baking gingerbread, a simple coat-hanger wreath is just the thing. And if you really love the idea of a minimalist wire circle wreath, you might purchase inexpensive metal floral hoops. I now have several in a pretty brass color, and they look gorgeous with just a few sprigs of greenery and a silk ribbon bow.

1. If using, take your wire coat hanger and shape the bottom into a circle. Leave the hook in place for hanging. Take your time and shape it as well as you can. It doesn't have to be perfect, especially if you intend to cover most of the wire with greenery.

2. Gather evergreen sprigs, like holly, boxwood, cedar, and cypress, as well as the dried flowers of ornamental grasses and hydrangeas. Colorful winterberries also make an eye-catching addition. Collect the sprigs into small bundles, securing each with floral wire or tape.

3. Attach each bundle of greens and dried flowers to the wire frame with more wire. Cover your coat hanger completely, overlapping bundles as you go, or add just a few for a minimalist, asymmetrical wreath.

4. Finish with ribbon and hang on a door or window.

WINTERBERRY

I don't have bird feeders in my yard, but I do have winterberry shrubs. They look especially beautiful in the garden when their berries glow in autumn and winter, and by spring they have fed innumerable birds. As well, the berried stems make beautiful additions to winter arrangements and wreaths.

Ilex verticillata is a deciduous North American holly. It sheds its leaves in fall, leaving behind only those bright berries. Winterberry shrubs with red berries are most common, but I love the varieties with berries in a lovely soft coral color, and I have even seen new varieties with sunny yellow berries. Winterberry shrubs like moist, acidic soil, and the plants are either female or male. One male plant can help pollinate several female plants, ensuring colorful berries for us and the birds.

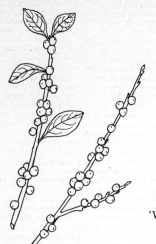

SCIENTIFIC NAME:
Ilex verticillata

COMMON NAME:
winterberry

FAVORITE VARIETIES:
'Winter Gold' (pollinated by 'Southern Gentleman'),
'Winter Red', and the more compact variety 'Red Sprite'
(pollinated by 'Jim Dandy' or 'Apollo')

THE WINTER
GARDENER

H ere is good news: almost everyone is a gardener in the spring. Even those who claim to have no green thumbs are seduced by the cheerful pansies offered for sale outside the sliding doors of the supermarket. Even those discouraged by a history of dead houseplants can't resist the springtime optimism of a new hanging basket of petunias for the porch. However, summer and fall are for the more committed gardeners who have learned to plan and anticipate. In summer, they not only water their container plants but give them a weekly feed. They deadhead and occasionally pinch their annuals back, knowing this will help the flowers to go on blooming. In fall, they dream of spring as they plant out tulip and daffodil bulbs. The committed kitchen gardeners bury garlic bulbs and imagine the bunches they will braid and hang in the pantry in June.

But who among us gardens in winter? We might tell ourselves that only the most intrepid and dedicated growers continue their work in the winter months. Certainly, some winter gardeners are of this sort. They live in icy cold places but keep their gardens going with polytunnels or hoop houses. Maybe they create "hot boxes" where lettuces grow above the radiant heat of deeply layered compost. Winter gardeners are also those who garden in warmer climates. Their winter is more like my spring, and they grow their tomatoes in gardens edged by palm trees. They pick oranges from their own backyard orchard. During the hottest weeks of summer, they leave their gardens blanketed with compost to rest, and they take themselves to the beach. Their seasons have the same names, but the rhythm of their garden year is different from my own.

I am neither of those winter gardeners, and yet my own winter routines are still shaped by my gardening life. Winter is a season of rest for me and my soil. My garden soil is given a break from actively feeding and growing plants. I am given a break from weeding and other physically demanding chores. But though I need rest, I don't want disconnection. The roots of my life are now sunk deep in the garden I am making here at Maplehurst, and it would be needlessly painful to pull them up entirely every time the weather turned cold and I shut fast the windows and doors.

Some sort of ongoing connection to the natural world is even more important during winter as we spend so much more time indoors and in the dark. Perhaps the easiest and most obvious way I maintain a connection with my garden during winter is simply by bringing a few of my favorite potted plants inside. The healthiest geraniums (which are properly called pelargoniums) from summer always come in to sit by the south-facing windows of my kitchen. If rosemary or mint is thriving in a pot, I bring it inside too. These herbs will never be as happy indoors as they were outside, but if I can just keep them alive till spring, I'll have fresh seasonings for my winter soups and a plant or two I can revive outdoors in early summer.

My winter garden is much smaller and simpler than the garden I grow in spring and summer outside the house. Details that might go unnoticed in July when so much is blooming are great gifts in January. In winter, after I wash the dishes, I take the time to rub the leaves of a scented pelargonium in order to travel, via the fragrance on my fingertips, right back to the green glory of high summer. The pale lavender flowers that appear on my Swedish ivy plant only during the shorter days of winter are almost more beautiful than an entire

flower border in summer. The low winter light that touches them through my bedroom window illuminates them so that they look like a buzzing cloud of fairies. This is one plant. The flowers are very small, yet sitting on an old stool by the window it is spotlit like a great work of art on a pedestal. It *is* a work of art. Every plant is a masterpiece, and yet it is harder to see individual plants in summer. In summer, we have the work of art that is the garden as a whole. In winter, we have one zonal pelargonium with its single pink bloom. We have one scented pelargonium with its resinous, glorious leaves. And we have at least one great ugly bulb prepared to astonish us.

A few weeks after bringing in the potted plants, I pot up an amaryllis bulb or two. The ugliest thing I have ever potted in soil may just be an amaryllis bulb. If all I had known of the amaryllis plant was its bulb, I am sure I would never have chosen to grow one at all. But first impressions matter, and my first impression of an actual, living amaryllis was rich color and diamond sparkle and my own, very great, surprise. We had only lived in our seashell-stuccoed Florida house for a few months when I cut through our narrow side yard and noticed the kind of spectacular reddish-pink flower I had only ever seen on a Christmas card. What was it doing blooming its head off in this slightly shady patch near my neighbor's orange tree? Granted, I was a new Florida resident, and the orange tree, with its pendulous green globes, imparted an equal measure of wonder.

Such marvels can only grow from the ground in very particular climates. People who live in real winter weather must content themselves with indoor gardening, which, as I hope I have already proved, is not second-best but merely different. Indoor gardening is difficult where orange trees are concerned but quite manageable in the case of the amaryllis. The advantage to this indoor gardening is that the gardener, and not the weather, controls the timing of the bloom, and amaryllis bulbs are often "forced" into flower in time for the winter holidays. So on a gray November day, a few years after trading Florida seashells for Pennsylvania brick, I found myself for the first time standing in our kitchen holding a great, dirty bulb. It trailed fleshy roots like an octopus trails arms.

By this moment, I had lived in Pennsylvania for a few years and was well acquainted with the usual fall-planted bulbs like daffodil and tulip and crocus. Those come shipped to me fifty to a net sack, like the bags holding onions in the grocery store. Spring-blooming bulbs are papery, like onions, and small—I can easily grab a handful of daffodil bulbs. An amaryllis bulb, however, is a two-fisted beast—as big as a softball. A bright light of fascinated horror shone in my young daughter's eyes when she spied that first bulb in my hands. We covered the monster in dirt, watered it, and placed it on our windowsill.

The history of this plant in the West is also ugly. Its introduction to Europe appears to have followed the same routes as the trade in sugarcane and slaves. The word *amaryllis* means "to sparkle," but when packed in crates in the dark holds of ships that also carried human cargo, I doubt it shed much light. My experience of the amaryllis's transcendent sparkle has its roots in the dirty muck of sinful human history and the fresh filth of my flowerpot. Yet for several winters in a row, I've watched as water and winter sunshine awaken a bulb that looks as dead as stone.

The name *amaryllis* is also linked to the Greek tale of a shepherdess who shed her own blood to prove her love. This is the story I remember each time I place our blooming amaryllis in the center of our dining-room table at Christmastime. The Greek shepherdess foreshadows our own Great Shepherd. And what was the world's first impression of Christ? A mother pregnant well before her wedding, an animal feed trough, a small and vulnerable infant. The mystery of the gospel was revealed to us in flesh that would bleed for us, yes—but that flesh came barefoot and caked with dust. It was not a good first impression, and if I had passed the scene on a dusty Bethlehem road, I may not have cared to look twice.

When the amaryllis bulb finally erupts with new life, the sight is astonishing but not exactly beautiful. A pale green stalk, the color of celery and the shape of a sword, pushes itself up. Every hour it heaves itself higher. One inch, then two, it is six inches high almost before you realize what is happening. When the flower opens a week or two later, what was once hidden is finally revealed. And what is revealed is the kind of beauty that drops your jaw and stops you in your tracks. You cannot help but look twice. And then go on looking.

Occasionally, I drop my spent amaryllis bulbs in the compost bin once their Christmas blooms are finished, but I have a few favorites I coddle in my cool basement in order to coax them into bloom another year. If anything, the bulbs have only grown uglier, but I no longer shudder when I handle them. Instead, I feel affection born of the care I have lavished on them and the faith I have in the beauty of their flowers. I have always wondered why such a glory and a gift as Emmanuel didn't simply appear, a fully grown God-man, trailing rainbows rather than clouds of dust. Would that have helped us recognize him? Perhaps not. Perhaps we have always needed exactly what we have been given, something mysterious as heavenly glory emerging from the dust of earth.

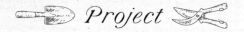

FORCING AMARYLLIS AND PAPERWHITE NARCISSUS BULBS

All gardeners, no matter their climate, can grow flowering bulbs indoors. Winter is the perfect time of year for amaryllis and paperwhite narcissus bulbs. Both make beautiful, natural Christmas decor, but I almost always appreciate them even more after the Christmas tree has been dragged out to the woods. Those weeks just after the Christmas season can feel a bit dull, but there is nothing dull about these flowers.

Amaryllis are huge bulbs that grow great big flowers—often four or more from a single bulb. I love the variety 'Appleblossom' with its white flowers striped with pink. Paperwhite narcissus bulbs are essentially daffodils that do not like winter cold. They don't need to be pre-chilled, and their small white flowers have a spicy scent. If you are not a fan of the strong fragrance, try the variety 'Wintersun' for a more delicate perfume.

1. Do not chill these bulbs. Keep them in a dark, dry place until you are ready to pot them.

2. Plant in regular potting soil without fully covering the bulbs, or grow them in water only. If using soil, I like to use a pot with no drainage hole, and I cover the soil around the bulb top with some pretty green moss.

3. For water growing, place clean pebbles or glass marbles at the bottom of a clear container. Place one amaryllis bulb or several paperwhite bulbs on top. Fill your container with water just to the level of the roots. Maintain that water level as your bulbs begin to grow.

4. Paperwhites can grow very tall. I stake mine to keep them from toppling, or I use silk ribbon to tie the stems together, which prevents them from splaying and flopping. A tall, cylindrical glass vase can also help contain paperwhites and vigorous amaryllis without the need for staking.

THIS PRESENT
(NOSTALGIC) MOMENT

ince middle school, I've been caught in an inner tug-of-war I can never win. I am constitutionally unwilling to follow trends. I value uniqueness almost above all else, and for too long the pursuit of "specialness" ruled me. And yet my preteen self (and still—some days—my fully adult self) shudders at the thought of appearing out of step with fashion. What's a girl supposed to do if she doesn't care to be trendy yet doesn't want to seem unfashionable either? Is there a midpoint between trendy and dowdy? If so, I've always been afraid that midpoint is boring and blah. And so the tug-of-war goes on.

Sadly, our personal Edens are not immune to the aesthetic dilemma of acid-washed jeans and leg warmers. Not so long ago, dahlias were considered by many to be terribly old-fashioned, but just like those acid-washed jeans, they are back again in a big way. Recently, I was flipping through a classic garden book from 1989 when I paused, suddenly realizing I was seeing something I hadn't seen in a long, long time: daylilies. Of course, I've seen actual daylilies quite recently. They are everywhere in municipal plantings, and I have quite a few beautiful daylilies in my own garden, but the stylish garden books published today and the new plantings I've studied at local public gardens do not feature great sweeps and masses of daylilies. "Daylilies," I said to myself, "are not in style." Perversely, that made me love them just a little bit more.

Dare I plant a great sweep of vivid daylilies this spring? Should I feature them in the new garden I'm planning for the partially sunny space around our big magnolia tree? Old varieties of daylily sometimes do well with a bit of shade. But I'm torn. It's the leg warmers all over again. I do think it is a sign of my growing maturity as a gardener that I am even considering bucking the no-daylily trend. Before I began growing my own flowers, I was a terrible snob about the cut flowers I would bring into my house and had too many firm ideas about the colors I liked and the colors I disliked. No orange flowers for me, thank you! Until I fell in love with tithonia. No boring carnations either! Until I realized how difficult they are to grow on my soil and began to crave them. And at Christmas? Don't even get me started on the red poinsettias sold in every supermarket. How predictable. How boring.

But are they? If enough people become snobs about plants, then the old-fashioned plant is special again. I had red poinsettias at my wedding because Jonathan and I married just after Christmas. I knew the church would be decorated with poinsettias, and while they weren't my flower of choice, they carried the distinct advantage of being free. I chose bridesmaid dresses in deep, dark green, and the final look was elegant and abundant in a way I could never have afforded if I had needed to decorate the church fully from my own small budget. But these days I *choose* to bring home poinsettias at Christmastime. My annual poinsettia purchase began because there is a family farm with a year-round market quite close to my house. In December, they sell boxes of citrus shipped straight from other family farms in Florida, and having lived in Florida for two years, I still associate winter with fresh-squeezed grapefruit juice in every lovely shade of pink. I first visited the market for grapefruit but noticed they also sold enormous poinsettias in red, white, and pink. Last year, I chose white (which is really more of a pale yellow gold, if we're being accurate), and it looked Christmassy and elegant on a plant stand at the turn of the stairs.

Another Christmas cliché I have embraced in recent years is the red rose. I don't buy roses at any other time of year, preferring of course to grow my own, but

Christmas is a time for indulgence and for special, once-a-year things, and a bouquet of ethically grown, long-stemmed red roses has become a special thing I add to my grocery cart each year when I do the big Christmas shopping run. A bowl of roses on a dark tablecloth and the lights from the tree dancing on crystal goblets— what could be more special? No one would mistake that tablescape for a summer barbecue or a springtime birthday feast. Everything about it says Christmas.

Which is ultimately the point. Flowers and plants speak. Are we paying attention? Are we allowing them to help our home tell a story? The red roses and the poinsettia are old-fashioned. They can be, at times, a cliché. But at a time of year when I want nostalgia, when I *want* memory and history to dance across my table, then a powerful, recognizable symbol like a red Christmas flower might be the very thing. I can always cut the sentimental sweetness with a fashionably wrinkled linen tablecloth in slate gray. The power of contrast plus the power of cultural symbols equals a very clear yet creative statement.

When Christmas ends, I study my new plant catalogs, including a lovely catalog devoted only to daylilies. They might not be the flower everyone is talking about today. They will never take the wedding flower market by storm. Sadly, their bloom-for-a-day blossoms don't really work for professional arrangements. However, they are still great for home bouquets, and a stem with a few buds will even continue to open over time. What, then, are daylilies saying to me? I have worried their message is "this gardener is out of touch" or maybe "this gardener is hopelessly old-fashioned," but the graceful heirloom daylilies in my catalog look old-fashioned in the best possible way. They look like a living link to the gardens and gardeners of the past. After all, when we tend a garden, we also tend our connections to a place and to a present moment, but no present moment is a disconnected moment. Perhaps holding on to daylilies, like holding on to poinsettias and red roses, is a way of enriching the present moment with more of the life of the past, and there is nothing dowdy about that.

ROMANTIC RED FLOWERS FOR CUTTING

From the time he was quite small, my younger son begged me to grow red flowers in the garden. He may have been tiny, but his desire for red flowers was large. Alas, his mother prefers her garden palette in purples and pastels. She makes her strongest color statements with salmon pink and coral. However, she *was* married at Christmastime in between two towering pyramids of red poinsettia plants, so she knows the power of a seasonal red statement bouquet.

Here are some of our family's favorite reds to grow for the sole purpose of cutting and bringing inside (or perhaps for the sole purpose of tending our family's romantic side).

- Red dahlia: 'Bishop of Llandaff' is the classic choice, a much-loved, dark-leaved, red-flowering dahlia.

- Red zinnia: all of the zinnias in the 'Benary's Giant' series are big, gorgeous plants that make stunning cut flowers, but 'Benary's Giant Deep Red' is the richest and reddest of the bunch.

SCIENTIFIC NAME:
Rosa 'Munstead Wood'

COMMON NAME:
English rose 'Munstead Wood'

REASONS TO LOVE IT:
This is a heavily scented and deeply red rose.

THE NECESSITY
OF WINTER

Trying to grow a garden in a place without winter was, for me, like trying to parent a toddler who refuses to take an afternoon nap. At least once a year during the period I lived in Florida, I sincerely wished my entire backyard would go away and leave me alone, for goodness' sake. Of course, the problem was with me, the gardener, not the garden. Without seasonal boundaries, it was up to me to be firm and gently put my garden to sleep during the hottest summer months. I learned this when I joined a vegetable share through a local family-run organic farm. Each week from November through June, my kids and I went to the farm and retrieved our bag of fresh-picked goodies. We'd find everything from kohlrabi to golden beets in glorious piles on the tables in a white-painted shed that stood at the center of a grove of citrus trees. In July and August, the fields of that farm were sown with a cover crop or covered in manure, and the farmers took their "winter" break.

Now that I live in Pennsylvania, nature doles out the rest my garden and I both need in the form of freezing temperatures and occasional snowfall. But what does it mean to rest as a gardener? Is it simply the cessation of activity? More sitting by the fire, less pulling up weeds? The answer is yes and also no. My body does rest more in these winter months. Shorter days mean I'm in bed early, when in summer I'd be outside watering containers or taking photographs of the garden with the last of the summer light. But the less physically active days of winter open up a space for more activity of the mind. In winter, I leave the watering can and spade in the garden shed and chase the *idea* of the garden. If I catch it, I'll be ready for spring. If I don't, I'll feel as worn out by the work of gardening as the parent of a toddler on a nap strike.

The *idea* of the garden is hard to define, not least because it is different for each of us. For all its vagueness, it is a powerful force in my gardening life. It is the reason I became a gardener in the first place. It is the thing that motivates me to keep going. After all, floral perfection arrives in my garden in May or June, but it only lasts for a few weeks. Our motivation and inspiration must spread its roots beyond this fleeting moment. It is the idea of gardening that I seek out all winter as I study garden catalogs and favorite gardening books. This idea is something I first encountered as a child while reading the classic Frances Hodgson Burnett novel *The Secret Garden*. The story of how Mary Lennox was transformed by the work of reawakening a long-neglected garden on the grounds of an English country estate awakened in me a longing for flowers. The work of gardening is its own reward. Mary is physically and emotionally changed by it. Personally I love it because it takes me out of my head, quiets my racing thoughts, and leaves me feeling more at peace with myself and with the world. But gardens exist in our minds as well as at the tips of our fingers and beneath our boots, and it was that dream garden in my mind that first nudged me out the door with a packet of mixed zinnia seeds in my hand.

After a summer of hard physical labor outdoors, I find that I am almost *too* physically enmeshed with the garden. I am as tired as the zinnias that have finally collapsed full of seed. Scratching my many mosquito bites, I ask myself why I do it. Am I crazy to work so hard? By summer's end, I am always discouraged because I have lost touch with the dream. I have lost touch with the longing for beauty that I first glimpsed in my reading and that set me on this path to a gardening life to

begin with. I used to feel guilty about my seasonal slump, but this past fall, I sat in my late-autumn garden with a friend who is herself a professional garden designer and small-scale flower farmer. I must have said something apologetic about the messy state of my garden, because she said, "Oh, don't worry. I'm aching for the first hard freeze. I can't wait for everything in my garden to die already."

The shame dropped from my shoulders as I laughed. Maybe not everyone feels quite this way about the end of the growing season, but the fact that some of us do is not a sign of failure. It is a sign that we have given our gardens our all, and we are tired. We need rest, and we need new garden dreams. We need to live without armfuls of flowers and baskets of produce for a while in order to long for those things again. It is the longing—that ardent desire—that will fuel us for the work of spring.

The key to reconnecting with the garden in our mind and heart is, for a while, to stop thinking about gardening at all. I give myself most of December to forget about the garden outside my house. If seed catalogs show up in my mailbox early, I do not open them until after Christmas. If by the end of December the thought of a garden still fills me with a slight sense of dread, then I keep that stack of catalogs closed until well into January. Most mothers have heard the advice to "sleep when the baby sleeps." I was never able to take naps, but I learned early on in my parenting to practice some version of this. When my children slept, I never allowed myself to wash dishes or pick up toys or answer emails. Instead, as much as possible, I used those naptimes to recharge. I would read a book, drink a cup of tea, think my thoughts quietly. It wasn't indulgence; it was necessity. If I didn't recharge, I'd struggle to power through till bedtime. And I often found that spending naptimes quietly and thoughtfully, rather than in frantic effort or numb distraction, opened up a space for me in which I remembered my love for my teething baby or tantrum-throwing toddler. A little bit of distance was often just the thing for allowing love to well up in me again so that I entered my waking child's room and lifted her from the crib like a gardener glad for spring.

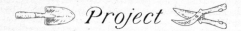
TEND OLD-FASHIONED GERANIUMS

Tending houseplants is all the rage again; even the macramé plant hangers have made a comeback. I am all in favor of filling our homes with green, but my aesthetic sensibilities lean toward the old-fashioned prettiness of African violets rather than the graphic modernism of a monstera. This is also why I love tending geraniums in pots indoors all winter. They look to me like something my half-Swedish grandmother might have grown.

Pelargoniums (or geraniums) are a common feature of Swedish interiors, where these flowering plants brighten up the long winters as they're coddled and cared for on sunny windowsills. I first admired them in the paintings of nineteenth-century Swedish artist Carl Larsson, who celebrates cozy domestic scenes with traditional pale, painted furniture, decorated wood stoves, and curvy longcase clocks.

Pelargoniums can be grown indoors year-round, but I keep mine outdoors all summer and then bring a few of the best pots inside to enjoy the sunlight streaming through my kitchen's south-facing windows. Because the sun is lower in winter, more of that light can enter these windows than in summer when the sun is so much higher in the sky.

Friends often marvel at my indoor pelargoniums, but my secret is simple: abundant sunshine and not a lot of water. I don't feed during the winter, and I make sure to let the soil dry out between waterings. Usually, I water once each week, and I remember to do it only because I always water on the same day of the week.

You can bring your potted pelargoniums indoors without any special preparation, but if I am taking extra care, I will pull the plants out of their pots, brush off the old soil, trim the roots a bit, and repot in a clean container with fresh potting soil. Then I cut the plants back hard, leaving just two or three green, growing shoots on each main branch. Don't be afraid to prune pelargoniums, and be sure to make new plants with those fresh green cuttings. Most will root easily in a jar of water. Like so many garden gifts, they *want* to grow.

PART THREE

SPRING

HUNGRY SEASON
AND SALAD ART

I read quite a lot as a child, but there were precious few books I consented to read repeatedly. The exceptions were The Chronicles of Narnia (oh, to walk in that quiet wood between the worlds!) and the Little House books of Laura Ingalls Wilder. It might surprise you that the particular Little House book I read over and over until the pages were soft was *The Long Winter*. Why not the seasonal farming rhythms of *Farmer Boy* (which I also loved)? Why not *On the Banks of Plum Creek* with its cover image of Laura frolicking on a green and flowery bank? The world of *The Long Winter* is so pared back and elemental. There is only the snow and the cold and the family's dwindling food stores. It's a story of survival, and I think, in a way, that brought me comfort as a child. It is also a story of the beauty that can grow in the barest soil, as the family persists in making music and reciting poetry while they wait for the snow to melt and spring to return. This is a book about hunger, but it moved me then and moves me now to remember that we must feed ourselves on more than food. Songs and stories, family and friendships are also necessary nourishment.

By March I am so hungry for spring I can hardly stand it. But I am not *exactly* hungry. Modern supermarkets keep most of us well stocked through the winter months, and we no longer keep an eye on our food supplies with growing concern as the days of winter pass. It might surprise those of us who find strawberries in our supermarkets all year round that traditionally winter was not even the hungriest season of the year. The phrase *hungry season* actually describes those weeks in spring when the weather has warmed but nothing edible has yet grown in our gardens. The hungriest season comes in that space between planting the seed and picking the first green salad leaf. Of course, hungry season isn't only a thing of the past. In some places, this hungry gap is still very hungry and lasts for far too long as subsistence farmers wait out the weeks, perhaps even months, before their next grain harvest.

These are the kinds of things I think about while planting viola seeds in winter. I may not have the answers to every global dilemma, I may not be able to alleviate all suffering and every form of hunger, but I can pay attention, I can be generous, and I can pray while I sow my seeds and in these small ways begin to weave my own life back into ancient and sustaining rhythms. I am partial to the heirloom violas called Johnny-Jump-Ups. Their deep purple and bright yellow faces are so cheerful on cold, early spring days, and once established in a garden they will pop up everywhere year after year. If I have a spot where I want them to grow, I place a small terra-cotta pot filled with them in that place. Once the flowers die and the seeds drop, I empty the pot and replant with something else, knowing I'll have many more Johnny-Jump-Ups in this exact spot next year. I understand that a beautiful bouquet of store-bought lilies might be the traditional choice when setting the table for an Easter lunch, but why not a terra-cotta container bubbling with cheerful violas?

It isn't only their self-seeding tendency that makes violas such generous flowers. Best of all, violas are food. Johnny-Jump-Ups are edible flowers, and they turn any spring salad into a work of art. Such delicate blooms might not sustain us the way a bowl of well-cooked grains does, but hunger comes in many forms. After months of winter, I am hungry for spring because I am starved for natural beauty and for time spent amongst green, growing things. To pick lettuces from my own container or raised bed (because lettuces grow so quickly and easily from seed) and to toss that salad with flowers isn't only a way to feed myself and

others. It is food as celebration. Food as acknowledgement of a new season. Food as relationship. As much as my children love a big, fat supermarket strawberry, it is the homegrown strawberry or the farmers' market strawberry—warm and sweet and just-picked—that grows connection.

Art is often perceived as extra, optional, or frivolous, but I learned reading *The Long Winter* that art is also a kind of food. Art comforts us like the warmth of a woodstove. Art connects us to one another through shared stories and melodies. Art is fundamental to our humanity. My preferred way to spend a holiday is in an art museum, but perhaps we have done ourselves a disservice by segregating art in this way. Both of my daughters love to sketch and paint, and both of them, when very young, asked me repeatedly how exactly particular works of art found their way into museums. *How does that happen, Mom? Who chooses? And why?* I answered them with descriptions of art schools and art galleries and art critics, but I wish I had told them the truth: the process by which art travels to a museum wall is unimportant because art is everywhere, even here, in this early spring garden, this salad bowl, and this shared meal.

Wendell Berry has said that "everybody is an artist."[5] His broad definition of art is especially relevant for the place maker and garden maker. Of the term *art*, he says,

> I would prefer to mean simply "the ways of making things." We have been using the term in the sense of fine arts, but when a culture is doing well, *all* its artifacts are made well and afford the kind of solace that only beautiful work can give .... If our ability to make things has degenerated to the point that we must go to museums to see art, then we no longer *have* art. Our museum is our mausoleum.[6]

If we want the arts to have a living, active role in our world, then the creativity we practice at home and in our gardens isn't optional, but foundational. What a gift to recognize that—with a little care and creative intention—the solace Berry describes is available for each of us, even in a salad bowl.

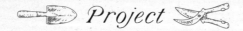

FORCE SPRING BRANCHES INTO BLOOM

The verb *to force* often shows up in garden manuals. The word sounds quite brutal to me, but no plants, animals, or small children are harmed in the process. Although, when my sons were young, they would often careen through the house playing or squabbling, and the fact that their eyeballs were on a level with my cut branches of cherry or forsythia always gave me pause. But still, no child has yet poked his eye out with one of my "forced" arrangements.

When we "force" a bulb or branch, we are pushing the fast-forward button, and the result is spring blossom and bloom before spring has otherwise arrived. We can force some spring-flowering bulbs to flower early indoors. Sweet-scented hyacinth bulbs are popular, and as long as they have had their weeks of cold (either before purchase or in a paper bag in one's own refrigerator crisper drawer), they can be brought into flower in a vase of water.

A single flowering bulb may be sufficient for bringing cheer to a kitchen counter on a snowy February day, but by March the landscape feels too bleak for one bulb to resist. The dark days just before the dawn of spring call for bolder measures. When the weather has warmed just a bit for a few days in a row (around 50 degrees Fahrenheit ought to be enough), and especially if the buds on some flowering branches are already beginning to swell, I venture out into the bleak Marchness with determination and sharp shears. The only difficulty comes when I try to slip back into the house with my arms full of branches just a little too wide for the doorframe.

I'm grateful for a wild old tangle of forsythia on the western edge of our yard. Forsythia force easily, needing little persuasion to open up their sunshine-yellow flowers in a big glass vase filled with water. Sometimes I shred or cut open the bottom of each woody stem to encourage it to drink. Ornamental cherry trees work well, and I especially love to take just a few branches from our venerable saucer magnolia. A single gray, twisted magnolia branch in flower looks like driftwood or petrified rock on which a few delicate pink butterflies have landed. Just about any spring blossoming shrub or tree is a candidate for forcing, though I am careful not to rob Peter to pay Paul by cutting out too much from any single shrub.

CROCUS LAWNS AND OTHER POETIC CONCEITS

True meadows are the unicorns of the gardening world—incredibly special and beautiful but also exceedingly rare. In practice, most grasses are much more robust than wildflowers, and unless the soil is quite lean and parched, grasses will grow and romp and generally crowd out the more delicate flowers. Growing our own meadow is a challenging proposition (despite what the instructions on those "wildflower meadow" seed mixes say), but growing our own flowery mead like the one seen in the famous late medieval tapestry "The Unicorn Rests in a Garden" is a much more attainable proposition.

Flowery meads were an essential element of medieval European garden design, at least if the artists are to be believed. A sort of stylized meadow, flowery meads were areas of cropped green grass studded with jewel-like flowers. The tapestries like the one depicting the unicorn were even called *mille fleurs*—or "thousands of flowers." In *The Decameron*, the fourteenth-century writer Boccaccio echoes the phrase in his description of a mead: "In the middle of the garden was something…even more commendable than anything else: a lawn of very fine grass, so green that it seemed almost black, enamelled all with perhaps a thousand kinds of flowers.…"[7]

A thousand kinds of flowers is an ambition perhaps best left for paradise, but those of us gardening in the cold winters of zones 3 through 8 (or those of us willing to refrigerate bulbs for a few months) can have our own early spring meads with crocus or other small, early flowering bulbs like *Scilla siberica* and *Ipheion uniflorum*. The effect is temporary, but then again, *all* garden effects are temporary. Simply plant your bulbs in autumn by the hundreds or—yes!—thousands right into your lawn. Thankfully most of these tiny bulbs are sold inexpensively in sets of twenty-five or fifty and look best planted in little clumps of at least ten. It is quick work to cover a good area of grass with these bulbs, and the more we plant, the more likely we are to see at least a few of our flowers evade the greedy hands of squirrels. When the bulbs flower, simply delay any mowing until the green foliage of the flowers has died back on its own. This is easily done as the flowers bloom so early. If we add bulbs to our mead each fall, we might indeed grow a thousand little gems of gold and purple. It is easy to believe in unicorns with such treasure underfoot.

SCIENTIFIC NAME:
Crocus tommasinianus

COMMON NAME:
spring-blooming crocus,
snow crocus, or Tommy

FAVORITE VARIETIES:
I love the straight species, but 'Albus'
is a beautiful white form.

HOW TO SHOP
FOR THE GARDEN
YOU ACTUALLY WANT

———————┼———————

Shopping for the garden you do not want is easy. Simply give your garden no thought all winter and then—in a moment of spring madness—fill the trunk of your car with every pretty flower blooming its head off on opening day at the nursery. Most of what you end up bringing home will fall into one of two categories: either you will have bought yourself an annual flower that will need regular feeding and deadheading in order to go on blooming (before petering out in early August from the sheer effort of producing so many flowers in so short a time), or you will have purchased one or more of the perennials known as *spring ephemerals*. These are wonderful plants custom designed by nature to flower in the bright light beneath deciduous forest trees in those brief, beautiful weeks before the woodland's leafy canopy fills in. To put it bluntly, your new garden will have disappeared long before the end of summer.

Perhaps I exaggerate. You might also bring home a rose tagged with a photograph of a very pretty flower in your favorite color, only to have it sulk and become diseased and pest ridden because the spot you have given it is shaded out by the house when the sun rises high in midsummer. Or you might bring home a spring-flowering shrub that looks like a scraggly green lump for most of the year. Yes, now I am just being mean, but my motivation is pure. I only want to save you from making the mistakes I myself have made. Thankfully, shopping for the garden we *do* want can also be easy. When you visit the garden nursery in early spring, you must spend only one quarter of that year's plant budget. Then visit the nursery again in summer and spend another quarter. Then—and this is the most important step—return several times in fall and spend the bulk of your budget at a time when summer *and* fall flowers are showing off, and the weather is just right for planting.

Of course, we are only two paragraphs into this essay, so you have likely guessed already that it is not always quite so easy, and there is much more to be said on the topic of shopping. I learned the hard way that the plants that look their best in fall cannot always be planted with success in fall. Ornamental grasses, like the cotton-candy look-alike pink muhly grass, seem to need a few months to settle into my garden in order to survive the cold, wet winters. This could be because they are only marginally hardy in my garden (pink muhly is rated only to zone 6), or it could be that they need very well-drained soil and it's my heavy clay more than my cold that kills them. But two autumns in a row I was seduced by their windblown pink flowers. They looked lovely until the first hard freeze, but they never returned in spring.

While shopping throughout the garden season is a good way to ensure long-lasting interest in our gardens, it is not, as I discovered, foolproof. This is where winter shopping comes in. Rather than visit a nursery when most of them are closed, or only selling tropical houseplants from their greenhouse, I let the nursery come to me in the form of catalogs. The better catalogs will give me all the information I need, including growing zones and seasons of interest and soil and light preferences, but even those that don't can be cross-checked with a good gardening book and an internet search. This means that a photograph of pink muhly grass waving its autumn flowers will lodge itself in my mind so that

CLEAR CRYSTAL®
LAVENDER
SHADES

when I see the same grass during a spring shopping excursion—looking like nothing more than a few boring blades of green suitable only as rabbit food—I can imagine what it will become and add it to my cart despite the limits of its juvenile appearance.

Ordering plants through the mail is also a surprisingly good option. I do this if I really have my heart set on a particular variety that may not be available at my local nursery in spring. I also like to order treasures from specialty growers in large part to support the work they do bringing new or rare plants into culti-vation that might never show up at our local big-box garden store. I have ordered everything from bare-root heirloom apple trees to small native prairie plug plants through the mail with great success, while so much of what I've learned about plants has come from reading catalogs. And yet, one reason why I love gardening and why I think more people should start gardens of their own is that gardening is one of the few activities left to us that really requires no shopping at all.

Visit the garden of a friend and collect a few seeds of *Verbena bonariensis* in fall. Help your neighbor weed her garden in spring and reap your reward with divisions of catmint or hosta. Honor your grandmother's garden by asking for a cutting from her prized rose. Gardeners are generous people because gardens are generous places. Most perennials need to be divided every five to seven years, which means their vigor depends on our willingness to dig them up, split them up, and then give them away, either to a new garden space or a new gardening friend. Perhaps the best answer to the question of how to shop for the garden you want is not to shop at all. Ultimately, gardens are not products, and human beings are so much more than consumers. We are cultivators and keepers, and we make our gardens with the overflow and the abundance of all that we share and all that we receive.

SUBTLE SPRING TREES

I grew up in Texas, where spring was announced by the wildflowers. Great rivers of bluebonnets would bubble up and flow alongside country roads and highways, and parents would rush to photograph their progeny decked out in sunbonnets and propped up in a sea of lupine blue. When I moved as a newlywed to northern Virginia, spring was a revelation of purple redbud, yellow forsythia, and white dogwood blossom. The pink butterfly flowers of the deciduous magnolias behind the Smithsonian Castle in Washington, DC, were only slightly less showy than the famed cherry blossoms near the Jefferson Memorial.

As much as I still love a blazing fireworks spring show, I have mellowed in middle age, growing to prefer the more subtle charms found in serviceberry, Carolina silverbell, our native fringe trees, and the Japanese snowbell or styrax. If you have always loved the ornamental cherry, why not plant a real, fruiting cherry? The flowers are much quieter, but if you're lucky, there will be sweet red fruit. If you live in the south, you may already be familiar with the charms of backyard citrus blossoms. These trees may not steal the show, but who wants a garden full of divas? I am more and more beguiled by the delicate flowers of native trees and orchard trees and those shrubs like daphne and deutzia that whisper but never shout.

SCIENTIFIC NAME:
Chionanthus virginicus

COMMON NAME:
American fringe tree

REASONS TO LOVE IT:
Pollinators and gardeners love its spring fragrance.

OPEN THE WINDOWS,
OPEN THE DOORS

———————|———————

A ll the best gardeners are allergic to their gardens," I tell myself as the nurse pokes the testing needle down into the soft inner flesh of my arm. This room where I sit waiting to receive the allergist's confirmation of what I already know—have known my entire life—is the very opposite of the places I love best. It is entirely beige, completely sterile, and there is no natural light. A faux house-plant would die in this place. In the waiting area just outside my room, there is a large aquarium. The only life in this medical office is the kind of dark, cold deep-sea life unlikely to cause an allergic reaction in any of us who live our lives aboveground in the sunshine amid the grasses and weeds and trees I love but that do not love me back.

I still remember the first time I heard the phrase *hay fever* as a child. I had recently been invited to an autumn hayride, and I assumed that allergies were a thing I need only worry about in the fall, but the fall held so many other delights—pumpkins and costumes, candy apples and hot chocolate—so hay fever did not seem like such a burden. I had hay fever, but I could live a life without hayrides. The next time I played with my cousins at my grandmother's farm, we could play hide-and-seek inside the house, or we could play with our fathers' old toy trucks in the soft dirt floor of the small barn instead of leaping from hay bale to hay bale in the field nearest the house.

As I grew, it seemed as if my younger sister was always sicker than I. She was the one who went to the hospital. She came home from the doctor's office with a nebulizer breathing machine, and I used it too sometimes, but it wasn't really mine. And then she started going in regularly for allergy shots, and I told myself again that she had allergies and I was just a little bit sick sometimes but really it was nothing. Sometimes I admitted to asthma in the office of the school nurse, who was also the school secretary at our small school, but the pain in my chest meant that I need not finish running laps around the soccer field, so maybe the pain was just my body's way of slacking off? I always seemed to second-guess and explain away.

A wonderful gardener I know is highly allergic to grass. Daily medication and forced time indoors help her manage the unmanageable. I once read that famed British gardener Beth Chatto was extremely allergic to most plants through long-time overexposure. She wore gloves or else suffered painful blistering. These thoughts comfort me, as if allergies are the sign of my belonging and not of my estrangement. And estrangement is the right word. My son was born estranged from the world and from my milk, and his whole body was angry with eczema. With each new food he tried, we discovered another incompatibility, but ten years later his body grew more comfortable, and one by one the food allergies— though never the nuts, never those still-deadly nuts—gradually passed away. But sometimes they don't pass away; they come on later in life, or as we age our bodies grow tired of always fighting them. Whatever the reason, early middle age has found me finally seeking out the same shots my sister once submitted to receive. A little poison is the antidote, apparently.

Every year in spring, I open the windows and the doors even though I know the pollen-thick air will make me sick. Occasionally, my health is bad enough that I retreat to my bedroom, windows shut, air purifier on high. But even then my version of spring cleaning has always been a simple airing out of the house. I can only imagine what has accumulated in the air trapped in this house all winter. Spring is for breezes blowing the lace curtains in the family room. Spring is for a sudden crash, when the wind through the back door causes the front door to slam shut. It's risky. I know that. There is tree pollen, my nemesis, on the wind. I will always shower at night after a day in the spring air. I keep our pillows and mattresses covered with protective barriers. Shoes stay outside. But our dog and our cat are welcome, and the doors and the windows are wide open; half of us are sneezing our heads off and the asthma inhalers are close to hand, but it is spring, and we are happy.

When the nurse returns, the long line of angry welts on my arm tells her immediately everything she needs to know. Allergic. To everything. More or less (more trees and plants, less animals, as it turns out). I take the medications prescribed for me. I will exercise and watch my diet and get my rest and drink my water, but I will also air out my house and keep on airing it until the summer heat slithers in and we retreat again, the thermostat set just so. And while I risk sounding like the fine print on a pharmaceutical advertisement—check with your doctor! Follow his or her advice!—my own advice is to open the windows and open the doors, though you sneeze and they slam. We need waking up after a long winter, we *and* our houses too. Ach-oooo!

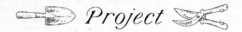

DANDELION CUPCAKES

Dandelions are a springtime weed and a superfood. They feed bees precious pollen and nectar when few other flowers are in bloom, and they can feed us too. One of my friends swears by the health-boosting effects of dandelion root tea, and I have a vintage cookbook on my shelf with a recipe for dandelion wine I've always wanted to try. The vivid yellow flowers are also edible sunshine in pancakes and cupcakes. This sort of baking is all about celebration. It is all about paying attention to the glory of the present moment. Strictly speaking, do dandelion cupcakes taste better than plain vanilla or chocolate? No, they do not. Strictly speaking, are dandelion cupcakes as easy to make as plain vanilla or chocolate? No, they are not. First, there is the gathering. Then, there is the washing and the plucking of petals. Strictly speaking, are dandelion cupcakes one of the prettiest and most memorable things you will ever bake or eat? Why, yes. Yes, they are exactly that.

The "recipe" is simple:

1. Pick a bowlful of dandelions, preferably with a young child's help. Wash well.

2. Separate the petals from the bitter green leaves.

3. Stir up your favorite cupcake recipe (a simple vanilla or lemon flavor is best), and add a handful or two of yellow dandelion petals.

4. Bake as usual.

5. Frost as usual. I recommend decorating with fresh violets or simply more dandelions.

PRACTICE RESURRECTION

———————|———————

My flower garden began with pencil marks on graph paper. Months later, it grew to life in the bare but sunny patch on the western side of our house. Sketching out a garden plan on paper before we pick up our spade is always a good idea, yet it doesn't guarantee success. I lived for years with a flower garden that closely matched the one I had first drawn on paper, but over the past few growing seasons I have begun to admit that my original garden plan was not a resounding success. The four large quadrants of the garden, with a round bed in the middle where the gravel paths would cross, looked very nice. The garden photographed well. But it did not *feel* right. Because the center of the garden was planted with a bed of hazy purple catmint, the paths that circled it led you in and led you right back out again. Unless you were headed through the door of the potting shed—the gardener's domain—there was no invitation to linger in this garden. Even the benches I had once placed on the edge of two beds had been rendered decorative rather than functional as the roses and grasses grew to cover them. And no one—not even me—wants to share a small garden bench with a thorny rose. What was needed, I began to understand, was a revision. The new design would not look quite as good, but it would feel wonderful. Or so I hoped.

Are gardens pretty pictures to admire or are they places to be? This is the question I kept asking myself as I contemplated something radical: tearing out the central planting bed and filling the entire space with gravel. The current design was beautiful, with its circular bed filled with soft purple flower wands at the center of the garden, but it wasn't functional. I told my husband I thought we needed to dig it out and extend the gravel of the paths throughout the whole space. That would give us enough room in the middle of the garden for a table and chairs plus an umbrella for shade. There would be fewer flowering plants, but there would be more space for us to sit and *be* in our garden. It is a measure of my husband's love for me and his faith in my design ideas that he simply said, "Yes. Let's do it."

Wendell Berry ends one of his poems with the imperative "practice resurrection." I love the idea of resurrection as something I can make space for right now. It's exciting and empowering to think that rising to new life isn't something I merely sit and passively wait to receive, but something I step into and take hold of. This is resurrection as a way of daily living. But while the idea of beginning to experience today the thing I had only hoped to experience on some distant tomorrow is exciting, the daily practice of resurrection is, it turns out, a daily sacrifice. Hopelessness is a dreary experience, but it doesn't ask much of us. It leaves us alone, though where it leaves us is not much fun. But the practice of resurrection is active and hopeful and built on faith. My husband had faith in me, but I wasn't so sure my idea was a good one. Was I willing to do the hard, daily work of transforming this flower garden when the outcome wasn't guaranteed?

Perhaps it isn't even possible to practice resurrection on our own. Perhaps it is a way of living that works best when we are living from within relationships and community. My husband was willing, and he has the dexterity with a shovel to back up his enthusiasm, and so we began. While he did most of the literal heavy lifting, I dug out and divided the catmint plants from the center bed. Having sliced them into chunks, each with a neat tangle of roots, I carted them in my orange wheelbarrow over to the mound garden I've been trying to

tame for years. The mound in our backyard is all that remains of what was once a large stone bank barn. The bank once guided wagons up to the doors of a second-story hay loft. The barn is gone now, and only the stones of its foundation remain, but the bank itself is still a solid grassy mound. We placed a garden bench at the top, and it makes a nice perch to view the entire back garden, but the weeds up there have always been out of control. I hoped that a new planting of aggressive catmint (*Nepeta* is in the mint family, after all) would hold its own against the vines and brambles.

This would be quite a tedious essay if I detailed the entire process of our garden regeneration. It is enough to say that several times a day, for nearly a week, I complained to Jonathan that the project was "a lot more work than I realized it would be." Deep digging and heavy hauling is just about the most physically demanding work we can undertake in our gardens. I wondered if we'd gone in over our heads. And since my husband was carrying most of the burden of the heavy labor, I especially worried that he wouldn't find it worthwhile. We engage in a lot of labor calculus in our home: with an old house in need of near constant repair, time and effort spent on one project always means time and effort we don't have to spend on some other needed repair. Had we made the right choice? Had I steered us in the right direction? Or were we only—painfully and laboriously—spinning our wheels?

During springtime in our gardens, it is easy to look around and believe we aren't simply waiting for resurrection but are living in the midst of it. And maybe that's why I longed for a garden to be in and not just one that made a pretty picture from the kitchen window. In the garden, resurrection is a predictable miracle. I can point to my calendar and tell you, give or take a few weeks, exactly when this miracle will emerge from the still-cold soil. I can tell you all about the last time it happened, and I can plan for my garden's future, confident that spring resurrection will once again follow close on the heels of winter sleep and death.

Practice resurrection: it's a galvanizing cry. Do I believe that death is not the end of the seed but the beginning of new life? If so, then what am I waiting for?

Today is the day to live the resurrection I believe. And go on living it. Because that is the thing about ordinary, predictable, life-changing miracles: they are ordinary, predictable, life-changing practices. They aren't a one-time-only happening, they are always happening. They are always inviting us to participate. To practice resurrection means living in ways that make resurrection possible. If I don't save a seed or purchase a seed, if I don't plant the seed and water the seed, then the seed can't die. If the seed can't die, the seed can't live again. What should I be losing, and letting go, and allowing to die? What dreams should I be tucking in for a long winter's sleep? And where and what should I be planting with hope and faith? Gardener and theologian Vigen Guroian explains that God calls us to tend "not only the garden that we call nature but also the garden that is ourselves."[8] I find that to be one of the most hopeful things I've ever heard. Because gardens—and you can take this gardener's word for it—*always* come back to life.

I gave up the perfect paper plan of my flower garden. I let go of the photogenic way the purple catmint softened the straight lines of the white garden shed. I wore myself out carrying heavy bags of pea gravel. And while I remember the doubt and the effort, the memory that is most vivid to me is of the first time we sat, Jonathan and I, comfortably, at our glass-topped table, right there in the very center of the flower garden. The roses weren't yet blooming, but I could see how they were just about ready to burst into flower all around us. It was my old, beloved flower garden, but it was new and improved and I was no longer an observer. This garden was no longer just a space for passing through, one that let me enter but then spit me right back out again. Now it had become a garden embrace. Have you ever been held by a garden? It's worth any effort, and there's simply no place I'd rather be.

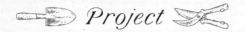

GROW YOUR OWN BOUQUET

I am easily seduced by every flower in the seed seller's catalog, forgetting that I really do prefer my indoor cut flowers in a fairly narrow range of colors. It seems like an obvious idea to plant flowers for cutting that you actually *want* to cut and bring indoors, but I am surprised at how I go on growing flowers in golden yellow and deep bronze, and while they look amazing in my garden, I never do cut them. The whole point of growing your own flowers for your own bouquets is to grow exactly what you like and want to have close by, and for me that means pinks and purples and anything with a delicate umbrellalike shape.

Not sure what you like or how to combine colors? Follow these suggestions for a cut flower patch you'll be eager to harvest:

- Grow several varieties of one flower. There's a good chance that the color tones will harmonize. Try this with calendula or cosmos. Bouquets of a single flower are simple and lovely.

- Assume you will require a lot more "filler" foliage than you think you will need. I almost never manage to cut enough "filler" when I first go out with my flower scissors. Inevitably, wild spring and summer bouquets require more. Grow your own from seed or take stock of your landscape plants. They often make great additions to arrangements and may even guide you toward a particular flower. Lots of hosta leaves? Try big and bold sunflowers or tithonia. Beautiful plum-colored ninebark shrubs? Flowers in pale pink will glow against that backdrop.

- Herbs, and even gone-to-flower vegetables, can make uniquely beautiful bouquets.

- Pay attention to shape as well as color tones. It's nice to have a variety of round, solid shapes; taller, spiky shapes; umbrellalike umbel shapes; and floating, vining shapes. The beauty is in the dynamic contrast.

CUT YOUR DARLINGS

There is a saying among writers that we must learn to "kill our darlings." It means we must not grow overly attached to a turn of phrase or a lilting sentence but must be willing to edit ruthlessly. I am a writer who holds similar values in my garden. Ruthless editing is a must for great garden design, though I fail miserably year after year because it hurts my heart to dig out anything growing vigorously and with abandon. Still, I acknowledge that I *should* do this. I also hold that we should cut our garden flowers and bring them indoors, but fortunately this tenet is one I find *fairly* easy to follow. It is only fairly easy to follow because committed as I am to keeping fresh flowers in the house for as many months of the year as possible, there is always the worry that my outdoor landscaping will be denuded by too much cutting. Truthfully, I want to cut my darling flowers, but only if on passing that border the next day, it would be difficult to say whether I had cut anything at all. I suppose I want a garden a bit like Mary Poppins's carpetbag. Simply reach in and grab whatever your heart desires without changing the dimensions of the bag one jot.

Fortunately, there are quite a few plants that welcome our cutting. Indeed, they long for it. Cutting cosmos and cornflowers, sweet peas and zinnias is the surest way to keep those flowers going. Once the flowers turn into seeds, their job—genetically speaking—is finished and they expire soon after. But what if you want a vase filled with once-a-year spring beauties like hellebores? Or tulips? Or peonies? Something that won't rebloom and will be missed? Which place wins the tug-of-war: outdoors or in? One solution is simply to plant more. Choose the size, shape, and location of your lawn and turn everything else into a border. You'll be surprised how much you can grow when, as my friend Julie Witmer is fond of telling me, you stop treating lawn grass like the flooring inside your house, laying it down everywhere without much thought. If you find pulling out the lawn mower as tedious as pulling out the vacuum cleaner, but love to create homegrown arrangements, turning sod to plantable bed is as easy as layering cardboard and compost right on top of that grass.

Having treated the whole topic as a problem in need of a solution, I am finally ready, three paragraphs in, to admit the surprising truth: you can cut *a lot* from most gardens and not miss it at all. Gardens really are like magic carpetbags. Reach in and pluck one red rose for the bedside table; it makes hardly any difference to the rosebush while transforming the bedroom. Shrubs growing a bit too full? Snip out branches and use them on their own or as filler in a bouquet and a backdrop for a few special flowers. Every year, I worry over whether to cut my peonies. And every year, I remember that three peonies tucked together into an old teapot offer a glorious show without making even a dent in what I call my "peony row." And this isn't the only magic at work. There is also the transformation that happens when we lift something up that we would otherwise view from far away and bring it to a tabletop where it can more easily be seen and admired. The daffodils that congregate all along our driveway and nod their heads in April breezes are wonderful, but even half a dozen brought inside and placed on the kitchen table cause my children to gasp and say, "Where did those come from?" as if they'd never seen a daffodil before, let alone passed a whole bank of them on their walk back from the bus stop.

Ultimately, this is exactly why we cut our darlings, both in books and in gardens. We cut our darlings because we love them and because they are so very precious. We gather and trim because words and flowers are sometimes like

diamonds in the rough. They need cleaning. They need shaping. They deserve to be set in bands of gold (or brown teapots with a chip near the rim). Carpe diem is much too relentless a philosophy for all four seasons of our lives, but it is the exact right thing for the fleeting perfection of spring. Friend, have you not noticed? Have you not seen? The waiting and the longing and even the still-too-cold days of early spring are finished: "Flowers appear on the earth; the season of singing has come" (Song of Songs 2:12). The daffodils are trumpeting, the wildflowers are running, the honeysuckle on the arbor is rushing toward the sky. When the first peony opens its ruffled face to the sun, then run, don't walk: smell it and cut it and bring it inside. Gather around it as a family or carry it with pride as a gift for your friend, but hurry, grab your scissors, open your arms—spring has come.

PART FOUR

SUMMER

ARRIVAL

---+---

The inspirational posters and T-shirts tell us that life is a journey, not a destination. As a gardener, I appreciate this emphasis on process. Gardeners, after all, are those who do the work of gardening; we find joy in participation as well as observation. And yet, while I can say rationally that the four seasons of the year comprise a cycle that repeats without ever slowing or arriving, my lived experience tells me something different. The first weeks of summer always feel exactly like an arrival. This is the moment I have been aiming for all along, whether I was digging up dahlia tubers in fall, reading garden books in winter, or frantically keeping up with the weeds in spring. I have journeyed toward this destination, and I *have* arrived. The fact that every year I want to stop time on the twenty-first of June suggests that some part of me wants a life like a great novel, where narrative drama finally resolves and the peaceful stasis of a good ending is reached. When the 'Albertine' climbing rose on the old split-rail fence erupts with its once-a-year blooms, I want to write *The End* in cloud letters across the sky.

We can't stop time, but should we try? That line about life being a journey is often attributed to the American writer Ralph Waldo Emerson. Hilariously, it is also sometimes ascribed to the hard rock band Aerosmith. Like so many popular slogans, it is a simplified and easily digestible version of an original thought perhaps related to these words Emerson actually wrote: "To finish the moment, to find the journey's end in every step of the road, to live the greatest number of good hours, is wisdom."[9] I love the ongoing process of gardening. I know that a garden is a work of art that is never finished. And yet every creating, working human longs for a sense of arrival and accomplishment. There is something wearying and demoralizing about the thought of working but never completing, running but never crossing the finish line, creating but never cleaning our paintbrushes and putting them away. I can't finish my garden. I hope I haven't yet neared the finish of my life. But can I somehow finish this exquisite summer moment?

I can make the attempt. I can try to leave nothing unseen, unnoticed, or unappreciated. In the garden, this requires a posture that can feel like a dereliction of duty. I may have my sights set on weeding beneath the rosebushes, but I must sometimes stop my weeding in order to cut and arrange a glorious bouquet. Few activities feel more indulgent, even wasteful, than creating a special bouquet for no other reason than to give it pride of place on my front hall table. I'm not exactly sure how long the blooms will stay fresh and open on the shrub, but it is certainly longer than the few days I'll keep them going in the house. And yet this seeing, this playing, this creating is the work of right now and should be attended to or else this early summer moment will not be complete. I will remember the bouquet all year. I can enjoy the photograph I take of it and frame and hang on my dining room wall. Art can complete things that would otherwise only ever be ephemeral.

In early summer, I also set aside time for frivolous garden crafts and recipes that seem like the opposite of Art-with-a-capital-A. Like the dandelion cupcakes of spring, these activities feel strangely necessary, as if this is the only way to seize a moment and stretch it out until it is spacious enough to step inside and dwell awhile. To do the thing that can only be done at precisely this time of year feels like a moral necessity, as if I honor the elderflowers that appear for a few fleeting days by turning some of them into elderflower champagne while leaving most to

transform into elderberries I'll later use for elderberry cordial. I acknowledge the beauty of the first roses and lilies by making flower crowns with the young children in my life. I honor the pink, perfumed glory of the once-blooming heirloom rose 'American Beauty' by turning a basket of petals into rose petal jelly. When my friend Amy recalls a Midsummer Eve party at Maplehurst when we made flower crowns with our daughters *and* our sons, she says, "I've never forgotten it. It was like a moment outside of time."

We are hampered in these discussions by an English language with one word for *time*. Madeleine L'Engle was the first writer who drew my attention to the Greek language, which, meaningfully, has two words for our one: *kairos* and *chronos*. *Chronos* is easy for us moderns. It is clock time. It is linear, marching time. It is relentless. But *kairos*, in L'Engle's words, is very different:

> Real time. God's time. That time which breaks through chronos with a shock of joy, that time we do not recognize while we are experiencing it, but only afterwards, because kairos has nothing to do with chronological time. In kairos we are completely unselfconscious, and yet paradoxically far more real than we can ever be when we're constantly checking our watches for chronological time.... The artist at work is in kairos. The child at play, totally thrown outside himself in the game, be it building a sand castle or making a daisy chain, is in kairos. In kairos we become what we are called to be as human beings, co-creators with God, touching on the wonder of creation.[10]

The seasonal or fitting time that is *kairos* is implicated in human creativity, as L'Engle explains, but I believe it is especially relevant to garden making. As a gardener, I quibble slightly with L'Engle's inspired description only because we gardeners are in tune with the spiritual *and* material dimension of time all at once. Gardening is an art that unfolds in time and across the seasons. It is like music in this way, and musicians, too, must not lose hold of the beats and measures of time. We gardeners are not checking our wristwatches for *chronos* time, but we are keeping a close eye on the calendar. We cannot grow our gardens if we disregard the movement of the seasons. *Kairos* time in the garden isn't only a sudden visitation, that shock of joy. It is also, and especially in spring and summer, an anticipated joy. I cannot force a perfect garden moment. Even watching closely for it, I might not see it come. But it has come often enough in seasons past that I expect it will surprise me again this year in the perfection of an iris or the taste of an alpine strawberry. To lose myself in making a bouquet or stirring a great bowl of elderflowers in simple syrup or gathering petals for jelly is to take an active role in welcoming *kairos*. It is the active choice to step outside of *chronos*, for a few moments at least, and do something beautiful and rather pointless.

Yes, pointless. I still have a dozen or so small jars of bright pink rose petal jelly buried deep in my basement freezer, yet I am tempted to make more. It turns out that rose-scented jelly tastes a bit odd on toast, though it's lovely spooned over vanilla ice cream. It is not exactly an all-purpose food. But the feel of the soft petals, the scent of the steam, the brilliance of the color. Yes, I will make it again. Perhaps. One day. For now, the memory stills my soul and slows my sense of time.

Project

FLORAL ICE CUBES

Rather than burden you with a freezer full of pink jelly your children won't like, I'll give you another way to freeze the moment. Gardens give delight, and what could be more delightful than a floral cocktail iced with a frozen violet? Or a glass of lemonade scented with lavender or rosemary cubes? Freezing edible flowers in a clear cube of ice is one of the simplest yet most surprising ways to appreciate the beauty of a flower right up close. Your guests might manage to ignore the blooms at the center of your table, but they will be forced to see the flowers in their glass. And helping to open someone's eyes to flowers? That is a better gift to them even than homemade lemonade.

1. A silicone ice cube tray with a larger square shape works best for this project. Larger cubes will also last longer in the glass.

2. Experiment with any edible flowers. Violas and the small flowers of scented-leaved geraniums are great options. Herbs and the flower of an herb work well. A small rosebud would be sweet.

3. Distilled water should give the clearest ice, but it may or may not be worth the fuss.

4. Fill and freeze each cube in layers in order to trap the flower in the center. First, freeze a little water at the bottom with the flower floating on top. Then add a bit more water and freeze until set. Finally, top off with water and freeze completely.

5. Enjoy, but quickly, before it melts.

SACRED INDOOR-OUTDOOR SPACE

I f you have ever stepped inside a Gothic cathedral—the sound of your footsteps echoing all the way up and around the vaulted ceiling, your neck arched back and your eyes drawn up and up and up—you have felt the power of sacred space. I do not think I could shout inside the Duomo in Florence or Westminster Abbey in London even if I were tempted by some great reward. The power of the place affects even tourists carting guidebooks and selfie sticks. Sacred places, like sacred objects, are those that have been set aside for serving or worshipping a deity. We call them *holy*, and we recognize their set-apartness. And yet this separateness is still rooted in the natural, created world. How many of us have stepped into an old forest and, lifting our eyes up and up and up, said to ourselves or to our companion that these are like a cathedral of trees?

I have never heard the cry of a North American elk with my own ears, but the celebrated "acoustic ecologist" Gordon Hempton insists that an elk call reverberates like a magic flute in the Hoh Rain Forest of Olympic National Park because that place has the same acoustics as a cathedral. This forest, he says, is his "favorite church."[11] Perhaps I will never hear the voice of a bull elk transformed by the forest canopy, but I have heard small human voices shaped into magnificence by the great dome of St. Paul's Cathedral in London. Recalling the Evensong service there, I wonder whether a forest is like a cathedral or a cathedral is like a forest.

I feel quite sure that those who first built the great cathedrals and worshipped in them would answer that question differently than we would today. I often describe the soaring proportions of the Pennsylvania forests local to me as "cathedral-like." I have even said that the old maple trees planted the length of our long driveway meet overhead like the arch of a great cathedral vault. But architects and historians would no doubt remind me that the proportions of Europe's gothic cathedrals were modeled on those once found in the continent's vanishing forests. Flying buttresses, stone pillars, and the pointed arches of the nave carved space in ways that only forests had formerly done. It is a strange irony that the act of building—great cathedrals and great ships—sent Europeans hurtling toward New World shores in search of the towering trees they had lost.

The Christians who built cathedrals were committed to the idea of cultivated, sacred space. And their commitment was tested over the centuries it took for a community to build one of these architectural masterpieces. Such commitment was fueled by an optimistic creativity and spiritual fervor, and I marvel at it when I read the histories of these places. I live in a much more cynical age, and I am not immune to the cynicism, for it has some reason. It is an understandable if regrettable response to contemporary life and experience. Can those who have known the enormity of deforestation, nuclear disasters, oil spills, acid rain, and climate chaos feel anything but cynical about humanity's interference with the natural processes of the earth? Even the seemingly smaller degradations of invasive plants and pests that make it difficult and sometimes impossible for our native species to flourish are enough to make you want not a deer fence but a human fence, one designed to keep *us* from ruining one more vital place. Understandably, there is a growing chorus of voices calling for land to be "re-wilded"—not gardened in the traditional sense at all. I believe that might be the best option for many places, but I don't think it is the only option we should pursue as we seek to give better care to our places.

I am a committed gardener, yet I am not immune to the tug of despair. Why go on gardening when we have often done more harm than good? Why grow ornamental plants at all? Why not turn our places over to the weeds? Setting aside the fact that many places, if left to manage themselves, would only become wastelands of invasive species, I yet believe that the idea of cultivated space has an intrinsic value worth reviving and preserving and passing on. We have tarnished the ideal of our creative potential with our overflowing landfills and our vast parking lots and even with our imported exotic plants taking over woodlands and roadsides, but we would be wrong to give up on human cultivation altogether. Sadly, even our attitudes toward our own "bit of earth," as Mary called it in *The Secret Garden*, are those of management and maintenance rather than creativity and life. How many of us look out at our lawn and see a chore rather than an opportunity? But sacred notions of place that have been part of human culture for thousands of years can help us renew our cultivation of the land, both in larger community-based efforts and in our own homes.

Perhaps you feel that the creation of a sacred place on par with great cathedrals is aiming too high. "Why isn't a hanging basket of petunias enough?" you might wonder. My reply is that a hanging basket is a beautiful way to begin. My own gardening life has its roots in the balcony window boxes I kept filled with petunias during long-ago Chicago summers. The key thing is to shift our perspective and give a proper name to the things we are doing and the place we are creating: we are cultivating beauty and life, and we are making a sacred place. Perhaps we begin with petunias, but when we understand what we are doing and why it matters, we will be more eager to keep an eye on those petunias, to water them regularly, to feed them, to trim off dead flowers. Why? Because they are alive, and they have brought more life to our back porch or windowsill. And we won't stop with petunias in baskets. We might add a wind chime, like a church organ played by the breeze. We might add the sound of running water with a fountain, or even commit to regularly filling a birdbath or saucer and bringing butterflies and songbirds into our space.

History teaches us that gardens have always been defined by certain shared elements, the first among them being enclosure. Whether with fence, wall, or hedge, there was a clear dividing line between cultivated and wild. Those lines may be more blurred for us today, and we might even intentionally blur them in our space by designing formal areas near our house that shift into wilder, more naturalistic designs at the edges, but regardless of whether we are personally drawn more to formal neatness or informal wildness, some sense of enclosure is vital. As humans, we find peace in areas that feel sheltered rather than exposed. Before we know it, we will have created a place that requires ongoing care, and thus we will have made a place capable of caring for us. Who would have guessed that the enclosed plot we once managed and maintained is now capable of maintaining us?

SHADE TREES

I've lived quite a few years of my life in the suburbs, and my current home, though it is an old farmhouse, sits right in the middle of a typical suburban-style neighborhood. In the suburbs, we are understandably fond of midsize, non-fruiting trees. Here in the mid-Atlantic region of the United States, we especially love ornamental cherry trees like those that grow so beautifully around the Jefferson Memorial in Washington, DC. We also love the pink-flowering cultivars of our native dogwood tree, and until recently, when they were rightly banned from sale because of their terrible propensity to invade our natural woodland areas, we really loved our ornamental Bradford pears. The spring blossom was lovely, even if the scent was rather horrid.

Now that I am responsible for enormous, aging maples, hemlocks, and spruce, I understand the hesitation to plant a potentially large tree. We worry about storms, we worry about our foundations, and perhaps we aren't even sure where to buy such a tree when the only thing available at the big-box garden store is more of the dainty, short-lived specimens we already have. And understandably, given our love of fast fashion, instant makeovers, and those reality home shows that take a kitchen from dated to stunning in exactly twenty minutes plus commercial time, we want our trees to grow *fast*. Thank heavens our forebears didn't take this attitude, or we'd have no stately shade trees at all.

In our fixation on fast, we've lost track of the simple fact that even an immature oak tree is a glorious thing. The northern red oak I planted a few years ago is now casting enough shade for a picnic blanket, a feature even my mature dogwoods can't offer. The right legacy tree for your home will vary by region, but with so many varieties of oak, there is likely an oak tree for you. Plant a shade tree, and your future self will thank you. Plant a shade tree, and your grandchildren will thank you. Plant a shade tree, and you will have changed the world for the better.

SCIENTIFIC NAME:
Quercus macrocarpa

COMMON NAME:
bur oak

REASON TO LOVE IT:
Bur oaks are tough and adaptable shade trees that nurture numerous butterflies and moths.

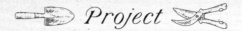

A FRONT-DOOR CONTAINER GARDEN

Some gardens (maybe most?) grow out of the compost of failure. Since moving into Maplehurst ten years ago, I have been committed to the ideal of two statement containers marking the steps to the front door. I tried quite a few plant combinations (meaning I killed quite a few plants) before I realized that my north-facing porch was simply too shady for dramatic floral displays. The kind of annual flowers that bloom all summer typically require a good amount of sunlight to fuel that much flower power.

Inspired by the porch decor I'd observed in our former Florida neighborhood, I shifted (wisely) to the humidity-loving, shade-happy greenery of two large Boston ferns. Initially, those failed as well, until I realized that the small pots in which they came dried out fast and the dry, congested root balls couldn't support all that lush green growth. I committed myself to watering the ferns every single day, and all was well.

Except I began to want more. Not just flowers and color but also contrast. Yet my ferns were happy in their well-watered pots. How could I bother them by repotting them in the company of other perennial shade lovers like hostas and heuchera or tender plants like coleus? I brought in a few potted plants from the garden center and set them near the ferns while I considered my dilemma, and that's how I discovered what should have been obvious long before: once plants grow full and are tucked in together, their separate pots are no longer even visible. I could give a distinct home to every distinct plant, push those pots together, and create the colorful, high-contrast front-porch shade garden of my dreams.

The floodgates of possibility had opened. This summer, I kept my two statement ferns, but I added perennial hostas, each in their own container, for contrast. The delicate fronds of the ferns up against the wide leaves of the hosta made both shapes sing. Still unwilling to commit to flowers, I added purple-leaved heuchera for color. I brightened the whole garden composition with the electric lime of coleus. Finally, I found my way to flowers. Wanting to emphasize the purple of the heuchera, I remembered my love for the tender houseplant *Plectranthus* 'Mona Lavender'. I've been growing this plant indoors since my Chicago apartment days, and it always flowers best in the shade.

In the past, I would keep it outside in the sun, and the leaves would grow luxuriant. I would then bring it indoors for winter, and it would shed some leaves before extending wand-like purple flowers. Suspecting that the plant only wanted shelter from the sun in order to flower, I added a few pots of plectranthus I had grown from simple cuttings kept in jars of water until they grew roots, and I finally had my flowery dream fulfilled in a spot where I had stopped expecting it.

Will I copy my recipe exactly next summer? Maybe. But I likely won't be able to stop myself from trying a few more experiments in color and contrast. With everything kept neatly in its own pot, fed and watered according to its own needs, front-porch gardening has become almost too easy. Someone might have to rein me in or I will give up access to the front door altogether. There's no need to walk inside, right? Let's just stand here and admire my brick-step garden. I think I love it more because it took so long to achieve.

THIS IS NOT
MY HAPPY PLACE

—————————————|—————————————

For all the months of winter, I keep my spirits up by scrolling through photos of my summer garden. In the photos, my garden looks like a perfect place. It looks like Eden. "It must be paradise," I tell myself as I move a little nearer to the fire in the woodstove. "And was it really so green?" Yet when summer arrives, the astonishingly green grass grows unbelievably quickly, so that I am begging one of my boys to go round with the weed trimmer (that I have always refused to call a weed whacker), even as the humidity rises and the mosquitoes take their first bite. What happened to paradise? This is ordinary earth with glimmers of Eden when I squint my eyes and look askance. Though sometimes, I admit, it is much more than a glimmer, as for instance when my children chase a rainbow that seems to point directly to the spot where I grow golden, pear-shaped tomatoes.

I cannot call the garden my "happy place," because I am not always happy in my garden. I am happy when the roses first bloom in early summer, but I am not happy when blackspot turns their glossy green leaves to sickly yellow. I am happy on the first really warm and sunny day in spring, but I am not happy when the humidity soars in summer. I am unhappy when too little rain leaves my mop-head hydrangeas wilted, and unhappy when too much rain flattens the dahlias I haven't yet staked. I am happy pulling weeds, for a while, and unhappy when my weeding fails to make a dent in the soft, green onslaught of Japanese stiltgrass.

Gardening is a lot like parenting—I feel tired, overwhelmed, and yes, unhappy for a great deal of it, but I wouldn't trade my garden for the world.

If gardening were a hobby, I might need to reconsider gardening as a hobby. Are golfers ever unhappy on the links? Do stamp collectors sometimes turn the pages of their album in frustration? Do bird watchers stand in the woods and regret picking up their first pair of binoculars? I can't imagine it. It seems to me as if hobbies are vacations from everyday life. They are the weekly equivalent of our annual summer holiday. They are a day at the beach. They are a Sunday nap. But gardening isn't a vacation from ordinary life. Gardening is the art of tending ordinary yet miraculous life. Gardening is a relationship.

To tend life, we contend with death. No wonder I am sometimes happy only up until the moment I step into my garden. My happiness can evaporate instantly at the sight of weeds or pests or evidence of my own neglect. Happiness slips away once the sweat begins to run into my eyes or the wheelbarrow I've over-loaded tips precious compost all over the gravel path. When the groundhog digs yet another tunnel into my flower garden, when squirrels steal every crocus bulb I planted last fall, when deer treat the yew hedge like a salad bar, and when I forget to bring the tomato seedlings indoors on the night of an expected freeze, I am tempted to throw my gloves under a shrub and head inside. There is death in the garden (*why* was most of my 'Lady of Shalott' rose winter-killed this year?) and there is even death in me (when I grumble to my husband that he never helps or I snap at the child who ran right through my flower bed).

Sometimes I do toss my gloves and head back inside. Sometimes I try to regain inner peace with a good book and an iced coffee on the porch. Sometimes I try very hard not to care so much. But the truth is I do care, and I don't really want a life untroubled by droughts and weeds and pests if it means I must live a life bereft of seashell-pink roses and dinnerplate dahlias and strawberries the size of my smallest fingernail that taste better than anything you could find in a candy

store. The garden is not my happy place, but it is my necessary place. It is the place I need, and it is the place my house needs. It is also a place that needs me, and it is good to be needed. It is good to live as a midwife for beautiful, green, glorious life.

We all need places for retreat. The cabin in the woods. The umbrella on the beach. The monastery in New Mexico. The adorable bed-and-breakfast in the quaint Lancaster County town. These are places where we can find rest away from our lives in order to return and better live our lives. But gardens, unless they are cultivated by someone other than yourself, are not places for retreat. They are places in which to dwell. To dwell is to root ourselves and tend our attachments— to people, to places, to particular shell-pink flowers. To dwell requires that we do battle with the forces of chaos that threaten order and art and with the death that threatens life itself. When we dwell, we are connected, linked to the people and places around us, and that can sometimes break our hearts (though connection mends hearts, as well). When we retreat, we are, for a time, disconnected. For those of us who follow Jesus, it is good to remember that while he may have gone off to think and pray, he always came back to share a meal around the table.

To speak of the garden as *my* necessary place begs the question for whom, exactly, this place is necessary. It is my conviction—perhaps controversial—that gardens are necessary for every one of us. No one is exempt. We all need food, water, and shelter, and I believe we all need some kind of vital connection to the ground beneath our feet. This is literally, materially true in the form of food. If we do not feed ourselves the life that grows, we will grow sick and we will die. But such fundamental material truths are generally true in other ways as well. If we cut ourselves off from the spirit of the God-created earth, will we also sicken? Will we also, in some way, die?

Of course, this is easy for me to say, living as I do in an old farmhouse with a few acres of land. My front steps alone have room for more container plants than I could ever have kept on the balcony of my third-floor Chicago condo. But my connection to a garden was nurtured even in that place by weekly trips to the neighborhood farmers' market. Though my student income was limited, I bought a single stem of scented oriental lilies every week for a month in summer because I knew that a flower in each room would fill my apartment with perfume for days. It must be twelve years since I laid eyes on him, but I can still see the sunburned, smiling face of the man who set up his flower stall every Thursday at the Hyde Park Farmers' Market on Fifty-Third Street. I think that man was growing more than he knew, for his lilies grew a hunger in me that has finally been satisfied in my own garden, where lilies were the first flower I tucked into the ground at Maplehurst.

A lily from the farmers' market. Pelargoniums in a window box. An aloe plant on the windowsill. A ready-made raised bed for tomatoes in the backyard. Such small, ordinary things, yet they nurture a sacred connection between ourselves and the dust of the land out of which we have been made. We might live three stories up in the sky, yet with a few plants to tend or a farmers' market bouquet, we are rooted deep in the ground. We have become not observers but participants in a cosmic story. Of course, we will not always be happy. But the happiness we do find is a deeper, richer happiness that arises not from the fleeting pleasures of distraction and escape but from our willingness to stay, to remain, and to tend our places in season and out, through winter deprivation and summer abundance, through autumn death and the resurrected life of spring.

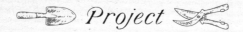

GROW A LIVING CENTERPIECE

A centerpiece for the table is a standard element of interior design. It is a design vignette par excellence. But what if we could bring even this familiar set piece to life? A living centerpiece for our table might be as easy as a flowering potted plant, cleaned up a bit and carried indoors. But with a little more effort, we can plant a living, growing arrangement, just right for the center of a shared outdoor meal.

Herbs and succulents are perfect for this. They don't need much soil, and they actually prefer a shallow container that might dry out a bit. A centerpiece of herbs is even edible. This summer, I have made mine by drilling a few holes in the bottom of a shallow galvanized ice bucket, the kind used for serving cold bottles over ice at parties. I used beautiful burgundy sedums and kept them at the center of my outdoor picnic table.

If planting up a mixed container with herbs, choose herbs that require similar conditions. Mediterranean herbs like thyme, oregano, and rosemary grow (and taste) very well together. Or plant up a shallow saucer-shaped container with multiple varieties of a single herb, like thyme. A big abundant bowl of thyme would anchor a shared meal beautifully.

COOL WHITE

The sizzling hot colors of rudbeckia, canna lilies, and other summer favorites fit the temperatures of this season well. But what if it all begins to feel *too* hot? What if you're looking for a reprieve from the soaring temperatures? It's incredible how the color white in the garden can visually cool both you and your space. I'm not sure I would believe it if I read it in a book (so I understand if you are skeptical!), but this July my eyes and my body have been drawn to one corner of my garden—the slightly shady edge where a row of white-flowering hydrangeas grow. That spot looks about ten degrees cooler than the rest of the garden, and I swear it feels that way too.

I've decided the trick is planting white on its own with a lot of cool, green accompaniment. White flowers are wonderful sprinkled in a border, but surprisingly, this non-color really can shout. Gathered up in its own space with only summer green around it, it's a visual bath of cold, clear water. 'Annabelle' and 'Limelight' hydrangeas work well for this. Anything that blooms white during the hottest months of summer is a good candidate. I have three white-flowering 'Natchez' crape myrtles planted between our brick house and black barn. White lilies that can take a bit of shade are also a good choice. Even better, plant a moonflower vine to draw you outside when the sun has finally taken itself off to bed. Double cooling.

SCIENTIFIC NAME:
Lilium

COMMON NAME:
oriental lily

FAVORITE WHITE VARIETY:
'Casa Blanca'

THIS SUMMER
HOUSE SONG

The words *house* and *home* are perfect synonyms. Even my youngest child knows they can be defined in exactly the same way. Yet young as she is, she also knows these words are not always exactly the same. This is why we have synonyms. One word is rarely enough for things that mean so much. House is universal because houses belong to everyone; home is particular, because home is my place. But then houses are also particular—*this house right here*—while home is general. My home could be a tent, your home could be a boat, but a house is a house is almost always a box of a house. Yet whether we are talking about camper vans or houseboats or little bungalows in the suburbs, we are really asking what brings a place—our place—to life. What allows it to become more than the sum of its parts? More than the black-and-white meaning of its dictionary definition? What makes a place not only *mean*, but *sing*?

As anyone with a passing appreciation for music knows, songs don't happen with only isolated, differentiated notes. The music sings when the notes flow, fitted together into melodies and harmonies and all the interrelatedness of complicated, gorgeous song. It's the same for the art of place. What brings a house to life? What grows a home in bloom? Connection. Interrelation. It happens when a house becomes a piece that fits within a larger puzzle. Sadly, we've forgotten this with so much of our modern design. Birds don't sing by our windows, because we've planted no trees and doused our green grass with chemicals. Pollinators don't buzz in our yards, because we've pulled out the clover and the dandelion. But if we plant it (or simply cease mowing it), life will come. To grow a garden is to grow connections: between the inside of our home and the outside, between our place and the wider ecology, even between ourselves and others. A simple herb garden means fewer solitary rides to the grocery store and more visits to our neighbor with gifts of lavender and homemade pesto. A soft patch of lawn grass near a flower garden will draw butterflies *and* neighborhood children. I have had small children march into my yard who, when asked, explained that no, they were not here to play with my daughter, but could they please go play with the butterflies? When one of my neighbors needed flowers for a baby shower, she knew to come to me. We chatted while we cut, and she carried buckets of flowers home that I would never even miss. And if those cut flowers *had* left gaps in the borders? Well, those gaps would have been more than filled by the conversation.

We live in an image-centered world, but the images we find online often tell us only a flat, two-dimensional story. Vignettes are king in the designed spaces we study online, and we should be forgiven for imagining that the perfect vignette is the pinnacle of good design. But in real, three-dimensional life, a vignette alone doesn't sing, because it is only ever a flat, observable thing. It is the thing we push aside in order to place our mug on the table or our feet on the ottoman. How is an empty vase placed with precision so very different from the same vase full of flowers? Why is one mute and the other musical? Because the flowers—even when we picked them up from the grocery store—link our interior space and our interior lives with the exterior world. They are not only signs of life. They *are* life.

With a little effort and intention, it is possible to fill our homes with the music of life all year long, but it is so easy to do in summer, we almost have to work to keep the life out. And as a mother of four, I have worked at it. I have complained about the puppy's muddy footprints and the pile of gravel—I mean, precious

jewels—my daughter has piled on the table. I have been annoyed when young children pick the flowers I call mine, and I have chosen not to bring a bunch of lilies inside because no matter how I trim the stamens, new flowers will open and drop their bright orange pollen everywhere. Life is just so messy sometimes. I know my husband has frequently grumbled about the fruit flies, which are our constant kitchen companions in August, when I insist on piling garden produce in every colander we own.

Clean and orderly are good things, but my sometimes tightfisted control is not. A home in bloom is beautiful but rarely pristine. A home in bloom is always growing and changing in ways I can't quite predict. If we want to see our homes bloom, we don't need to decorate. We simply need to live. Cut the lilies we grew even if something becomes pollen stained. Make the bouquet even though we'll be picking up browned petals in a few days. Dig in and plant some seeds in that space between house and home. Sing a song and let the flowers sing theirs. Flowers are blooming; the season of singing has come. Did you know the word *enchanted* holds the Latin word *cantare* inside of it? That small seed of a Latin word means "to sing." There are those with a natural talent for music, but I am not one of them. I suppose there are those with a natural talent for horticulture, but I am not sure I am one of them either. But it hardly matters when the abundance of life—not the stasis of perfection—is the goal. The earth is singing a beautiful song. Why don't we open our doors and sing along?

NOTES

1   Wendell Berry, "How to Be a Poet," in *Poetry*, January 2001, p. 270.

2   Christopher Alexander, *The Timeless Way of Building* (Oxford: Oxford University Press, 1979), pp. 8, 17, 25, 224.

3   Christopher Alexander, "Making the Garden," *First Things*, February 2016, https://www.firstthings.com/article/2016/02/making-the-garden.

4   C.S. Lewis, *Surprised by Joy: The Shape of My Early Life* (New York: Harcourt Brace Jovanovich, 1984), p. 7.

5   Wendell Berry, *Sex, Economy, Freedom & Community* (New York: Pantheon Books, 1993), p. 110.

6   Morris Allen Grubbs, ed., *Conversations with Wendell Berry* (Jackson, MI: University Press of Mississippi, 2007), p. 53.

7   Giovanni Boccaccio, *The Decameron*, trans. Cormac Ó Cuilleanáin (Ware, UK: Wordsworth Editions Limited, 2004), p. 184.

8   Vigen Guroian, *Inheriting Paradise: Meditations on Gardening* (Grand Rapids, MI: Eerdmans, 1999), pp. 9-10.

9   Ralph Waldo Emerson, *Essays and Lectures* (New York: Library of America, 1983), pp. 478-79.

10 Madeleine L'Engle, *Walking on Water: Reflections on Faith and Art* (New York: Farrar, Straus and Giroux, 1995), p. 98.

11 Krista Tippett, "Gordon Hempton: Silence and the Presence of Everything," from the podcast *On Being with Krista Tippett*, December 30, 2021, https://onbeing.org/programs/gordon-hempton-silence-and-the-presence-of-everything/.

PLANT LIST

———————+———————

pp. 2-3: *Verbascum* 'Southern Charm', lace flower (*Orlaya grandiflora*), *Rosa* 'Gentle Hermione', *Rosa* 'Sombreuil', Sicilian honey garlic (*Allium bulgaricum*)

p. 4: Lenten roses (*Helleborus*, varieties unknown)

p. 7: bronze fennel (*Foeniculum vulgare*), sage (*Salvia officinalis*), ninebark (*Physocarpus opulifolius* 'Summer Wine'), tulip 'Dream Touch'

p. 8: cosmos 'Purity'

p. 11: *Rosa* 'Queen of Sweden', *Verbena bonariensis*

p. 12: aster (variety unknown)

p. 15: Japanese anemone (variety unknown)

p. 16: zonal geranium (*Pelargonium* 'Classic Pink Blush')

pp. 18-19: Japanese anemone 'Honorine Jobert'

p. 20: peegee hydrangea (*Hydrangea paniculata* 'Grandiflora')

p. 28: ball form dahlia (variety unknown)

p. 31 dahlia 'Café au Lait'

p. 32: mixed dahlias, including 'Crème de Cassis'

p. 35 mixed Dahlias, including (upper left) 'Café au Lait'

p. 38: mixed hosta, purple fountain grass, Swedish ivy, *Plectranthus* 'Mona Lavender'

p. 41: upper left: prairie dropseed (*Sporobolus heterolepis*); upper right: *Miscanthus sinensis* 'Morning Light'; bottom: white yarrow (*Achillea*) and purple fountain grass (*Pennisetum setaceum* 'Rubrum')

p. 42: prairie dropseed (*Sporobolus heterolepis*), boxwood ('Buxus NewGen Independence')

p. 45: *Verbena bonariensis* seedheads

p. 46: peegee hydrangea (*Hydrangea paniculata* 'Grandiflora')

p. 53: *Rosa* 'Lady of Shalott'

p. 54: *Rosa* 'Distant Drums'

p. 57: mixed dahlias, including 'Verrone's Obsidian'

pp. 62-63: winterberry (*Ilex verticillata* 'Winter Gold')

p. 71: *Miscanthus sinensis* 'Morning Light'

p. 72: witch hazel (*Hamamelis* x *intermedia* 'Jelena')

p. 82: winterberry (*Ilex verticillate* 'Winter Gold')

p. 84: star jasmine (*Jasminum polyanthum*), rex begonia

p. 87: zonal geranium (*Pelargonium* 'Classic Pink Blush')

p. 88: Swedish ivy (*Plectranthus*)

p. 91: amaryllis 'Apple Blossom'

p. 92: amaryllis 'Dancing Queen'

p. 95: paperwhite narcissus 'Wintersun'

p. 96: daylily (*Hemerocallis* 'American Revolution')

p. 102: *Rosa* 'Munstead Wood'

p. 107: French pussy willow (*Salix caprea*)

p. 108: snowdrops (*Galanthus* 'Sam Arnott')

pp. 112-113: snapdragon 'Chantilly Light Salmon'

p. 114: hyacinth (unknown variety)

p. 117: Johnny-Jump-Ups (*Viola tricolor*), daffodil 'Moonlight Sensation'

p. 129: viola 'Gem Apricot Antique'

p. 132: sargent crabapple (*Malus sargentii* 'Tina')

p. 140: catmint (*Nepeta* 'Walker's Low')

p. 143: *Rosa* 'Lady of Shalott'

p. 144: foxglove (*Digitalis purpurea* 'Apricot Beauty')

p. 147: Mexican feathergrass in containers (*Nassella tenuissima*)

p. 150: Lenten roses (*Helleborus*), grape hyacinths (*Muscari*), hyacinth (unknown variety), *Viburnum tinus*

p. 153: white campion, peony 'Moonstone'

pp. 156-157: *Rosa* 'Lark Ascending'

p. 158: *Verbascum* 'Southern Charm', lace flower (*Orlaya grandiflora*), *Rosa* 'Gentle Hermione', *Rosa* 'Sombreuil', Sicilian honey garlic (*Allium bulgaricum*)

p. 162: *Rosa* 'Lady of Shalott'

p. 165: *Verbascum* 'Southern Charm', *Rosa* 'Gentle Hermione', Sicilian honey garlic (*Allium bulgaricum*), ninebark 'Summer Wine' (*Physocarpus opulifolius*)

p. 172: bronze fennel (*Foeniculum vulgare*)

p. 175: *Pennisetum* 'Foxtrot'

p. 177: *Rosa* 'Albertine'

p. 180: Chocolate lace flower (*Daucus carota* 'Dara'), *Phlox paniculata* 'Jeana'

p. 184: Shasta daisy (*Leucanthemum* x *superbum* 'Becky')

p. 187: lily 'Casa Blanca'

p. 190: clockwise from top left: orlaya, alyssum, 'Casa Blanca' lily, panicle hydrangea

p. 198: *Rosa* 'Queen of Sweden'

ABOUT THE
AUTHOR

———————+———————

Christie Purifoy is a writer and gardener who loves to grow flowers and community. She is the author of *Garden Maker: Growing a Life of Beauty and Wonder with Flowers, Roots and Sky: A Journey Home in Four Seasons,* and *Placemaker: Cultivating Places of Comfort, Beauty, and Peace.*

Christie earned a PhD in English literature from the University of Chicago but eventually traded the classroom for an old Pennsylvania farmhouse called Maplehurst, where, along with her husband and four children, she welcomes frequent guests to the Maplehurst Black Barn.

JOIN THE BLACK BARN GARDEN CLUB

————————+————————

Whether you are an aspiring gardener or an experienced one, Christie would love to welcome you into the Black Barn Garden Club, an online membership community committed to cultivating wonder at www.blackbarngardenclub.com. You can also learn more about Christie at www.christiepurifoy.com or connect with her and discover more about life at Maplehurst on Instagram @christiepurifoy and @maplehurstgardens.

With her longtime friend and fellow writer Lisa-Jo Baker, Christie hosts the *Out of the Ordinary* podcast where they help listeners grow a daily life that matters. New episodes are shared each Wednesday.

Together, Christie and Lisa-Jo and a community known as the Black Barn Collective turn social media's usual ways upside down through quiet weekly rhythms of listening, sharing, and celebrating in a virtual gathering place called the Black Barn Online. You are invited to join them at www.blackbarnonline .com and help tend a space where art and faith cultivated in a community take root, flourish, and grow.

BRING A LITTLE BIT OF
HEAVEN DOWN TO EARTH

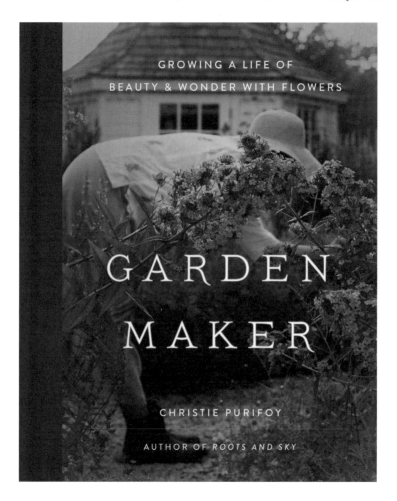

GROWING A LIFE OF
BEAUTY & WONDER WITH FLOWERS

GARDEN
MAKER

CHRISTIE PURIFOY

AUTHOR OF *ROOTS AND SKY*

Do you long to experience more splendor in your life?
Christie shows you how you can grow some of your very own.

Dig deeper at gardenmakerbook.com.